WHO DO YOU THINK YOU ARE?

EMBRACE THE POWER OF GOD'S WORD TO OVERCOME DESTRUCTIVE THOUGHTS. DEEPER SPIRITUAL AWARENESS, HARNESS THE HEALING POWER OF SCRIPTURES, AND THRIVE AMID LIFE'S STORMS

LORIE EUBANK

CONTENTS

INTRODUCTION

 *"For I know the plans I have for you, declares the Lord, plans for welfare and not for evil, to give you a future and a hope."*

—JEREMIAH 29:11 NLT

In Jeremiah 29:11, we find a comforting assurance from the Lord that He has plans for our lives—plans that are intended for our good and not for evil. This verse reminds us that God's intention for us is to have a future filled with hope.

The road to discovering who you are can be an endless and challenging endeavor, as it requires us to look deep within ourselves, confronting our fears, doubts, and insecurities. It often involves stepping outside of our comfort zones and embracing new experiences and perspectives. This journey may lead us to question our beliefs, reevaluate our priorities, and make courageous decisions.

Amidst the uncertainties and difficulties, we encounter along the way, we can find solace in the knowledge that God is with us, guiding us toward a brighter future. He knows His plans for us, which extend beyond our immediate circumstances and trials. His purpose for us encompasses our personal growth, the fulfillment of our potential, and the realization of our unique gifts and talents.

While the journey of self-discovery may be filled with twists and turns, it is ultimately a transformative process that leads to personal growth and the fulfillment of our God-given potential. It is a pathway to a better future—one where we can live authentically, pursue our passions, and make a meaningful difference in the lives of others.

I want you to know that you are not alone in struggling to receive and experience God's love. It is a common challenge that many of us face in our lives. I understand that past experiences, feelings of unworthiness, or distorted beliefs about love and acceptance can create barriers to truly comprehending and accepting God's unconditional love for you.

Perhaps you have been hurt by others in the past, leaving you feeling guarded and hesitant to open your heart to God's love. Or maybe you carry the weight of mistakes and shortcomings, believing they disqualify you from receiving God's love and forgiveness. These feelings of unworthiness can cloud your perception and make it difficult to embrace the depth of God's love for you fully.

But let me assure you that God's love knows no bounds. It surpasses human understanding and transcends our flaws and failures. God's love is pure, unwavering, and unconditional. It is not based on what you have done or who you think you should be. It is a gift freely given to you, just as you are.

I encourage you to take a step towards receiving God's love by opening your heart in vulnerability and surrender. Let yourself relinquish your burdens and trust God's forgiveness and grace. Seek a deeper understanding of God's character through prayer, meditation, and studying His Word. Surround yourself with a supportive community of believers who can journey with you and remind you of God's unfailing love.

In the pages of this book, you will discover the keys to living a more meaningful life—a life aligned with your true purpose and walking in God's plans for you. It is a journey of self-discovery, guided by the wisdom and truths found in the Word of God.

Within these chapters, you will uncover valuable insights and practical guidance to overcome the obstacles that hinder your ability to embrace God's plans for your life fully. You will explore the depths of God's love and learn how to receive and experience it in a profound and transformative way.

Through inspiring stories, biblical principles, and thought-provoking exercises, this book will empower you to confront your past, release feelings of unworthiness, and renew your mind with the truth of God's acceptance and grace.

As you read through the pages of this book, learning to forgive as we have been forgiven, you will be set free from the shackles of resentment and bitterness. Just as God extends His abundant forgiveness to us, we are called to extend that same grace to others. Through the example of Christ, who forgave even those who crucified Him, we find the strength and inspiration to forgive. We develop a humble and compassionate heart by acknowledging the depth of our sins and the immeasurable mercy bestowed upon us. Forgiveness is not easy, but it is a choice that leads to healing and restoration. As we release the burden of unforgiveness, we make space for love, peace, and reconciliation to flourish in our relationships. It is a beautiful act of obedience, reflecting the transformative power of God's forgiveness in our lives.

We must recognize that negative self-talk can be a relentless adversary, chipping away at our self-worth and hindering our progress. However, the Word of God has the power to dismantle these destructive patterns and replace them with the truth of our identity in Christ. By immersing ourselves in God's Word, we find a wealth of affirmations that combat the lies we tell ourselves. Scriptures remind us that we are fearfully and wonderfully made, chosen, beloved, and empowered by the Holy Spirit. They speak of God's faithfulness, grace, and unconditional love. As we meditate on these truths and allow them to permeate our minds, negative self-talk loses its grip, and we are equipped to speak life-giving words over ourselves. With the Word of God as our shield and sword, we can conquer negative self-talk, embrace our true worth, and live confidently in the knowledge that we are deeply loved and cherished by our Heavenly Father.

Remember, God desires a genuine relationship with you. He longs for you to experience the fullness of His love and acceptance. Embrace the truth that you are worthy of God's love simply because you are His creation. Let His love fill the empty spaces within you and bring healing to your soul. You are cherished, valued, and deeply loved by God. May you find the courage to open your heart and receive the abundance of His love that is waiting for you.

1

EMBRACING YOUR JOURNEY OF DISCOVERY

"For you created my inmost being you knit me together in my mother's womb. I praise you because I am fearfully and wonderfully made; your works are wonderful; I know that full well."

— PSALM 139:13-14 NIV

THE JOURNEY OF DISCOVERING YOU

To know and to understand that you are fearfully and wonderfully made, that there are no mistakes in who you were created to be, is to know your Creator. To know the One who created you in His image, to have a relationship with the Almighty. Adam and Eve had this relationship with the Lord. They were the first people created by God. They were the first to walk in fellowship with Him in the garden. God walked and talked with them in the cool of the day.

In Genesis 1:31, after creating man in His own image, and giving them dominion over all living things, the fish of the sea, the birds of the air, and all animals great and small that walked the face of the earth, He looked at all that He had made said it was very good. He Created you in His image. He knew what He was doing. He does not see any part of you as a mistake. If we are going to begin this journey to discover who you indeed are, we first must see what He says about you in His word.

It is essential that we look to God's word to understand what He says about us as His creation. If we do not start with His word as our foundation, then we will be subject to the lies of the enemy. And believe me; we do have an enemy that wants to steal, kill, and destroy. He wants to destroy the way you feel about yourself by telling you lies according to social media, magazines, television, and every other form of so-called entertainment. If you do not know what God's word says about you, it is easy to be fooled. The enemy can simply twist the words and plant seeds of doubt in your mind.

Look what happened to Eve in the garden. Satan, the serpent, was subtle and cunning and asked Eve, "Has God indeed said, you shall not eat of every tree of the garden." (Gen. 3:1) Satan caused Eve to doubt what God said by asking, "Is it true?." When Eve responded, she said, "We may eat the fruit of the trees of the garden, but the fruit of the tree which is in the middle of the garden God has said You shall not eat it, nor shall you touch it, or you will die.

Her response shows that she did not know exactly what God said. When God gave this command, He gave it to Adam before Eve was created. So, it is probably fair to say that Adam shared this information with Eve. Because Eve did not know God's word for herself, Satan was able to twist what God said and deceive her. He told her that God just did not want her to know good and evil because, in doing so, she would be like God. Through the seed of deception, she was tempted and saw that the tree was good for food and that it was pleasant to the eyes and desirable to make one wise. So, she ate from the tree and gave some to Adam. And immediately, their eyes were open.

Before this moment, they were never aware of their nakedness. They never knew shame. Suddenly as their eyes were opened, they knew they were naked, and they hid. What I say next is said in absolute love and not out of judgment. They both had a choice, they had free will, and they had no reason not to trust that God wanted the best for them. Unfortunately, due to the lies and deception of Satan, our greatest enemy, they made a wrong choice. And because they made the wrong choice, the course of mankind was forever redirected, to put it mildly.

When we spend time reading our Bibles, we learn who God is and how much He loves us. As I tell my children, when we read through our Bibles every year, we may be reading the same thing over again, but we always get something fresh from His word if we go into it, desiring to know Him better. Case in point, the text I mentioned above in Genesis. I never recognized previously in reading those verses that Eve did not say the same thing God told Adam. I never realized that Eve did not know God's word for herself. How can anyone be expected to understand what someone says without hearing it from the source? The same is true with our relationship with God. If we are not spending time reading His Word, how can we be expected to know what He has said about us, His creation, and His children?

Look at the scriptures above and recognize another point of Satan's deception. We know in Genesis 1 that God created man in his own image; he created them both male and female and then said it was very good. So not only did Satan lie and twist God's word about the fruit from the tree of knowledge, but he also made Eve doubt who she was. The deception in the garden was also used to make us doubt who we are. God said we were made in his image. But Satan convinced Eve she could be **like** God if she ate the fruit. She was already like God because she was made in His image. But Satan, the father of lies, planted doubt in her mind by telling her it would take that fruit to make her like God.

You must remember Satan, Lucifer, is a fallen angel. Pride got in his way, and he wanted to be above God. As he fell out of place and out of favor with God, he is on a mission to destroy all mankind. Just like he went after Jesus before He began His ministry on the earth, he is going to go after anyone who is committed to a relationship with God.

Beloved, hear me now; God LOVES you. You were created in His image, and He paid the ultimate price to restore a relationship with you through His Son, Jesus. The authority Adam and Eve gave away in the garden was given back to you through the death and resurrection of Jesus.

> "Who for the joy that was set before Him, He endured the cross, despising the shame…" (Hebrews 12:2 NKJV)

You are the joy this verse is declaring. He despised the shame that came with the price of sin, which was death. He despised the sin, not the sinner. He loved the sinner; that is why he endured all that he endured. He knew it would take His Blood to once and for all forgive all sin.

THE IMPORTANCE OF KNOWING WHO YOU ARE

> "And do not be conformed to this world, but be transformed by the renewing of your mind, that you may prove what is that good and acceptable and perfect will of God. For I say through the grace given to me, to everyone who is among you, do not think of himself more highly than he ought to think, but to

think soberly as God has dealt to each one a measure of faith." Romans 12:2-3

We must renew our minds through the Word of God to not conform to this world. God does not want you to see yourself as the world sees you. He wants you to see yourself as He sees you. I will give you an example of the difference between the Word and the World. It is a simple thin line. Take a look.

WORD   WORLD

Do you see that? A simple thin line. To be clear, it is the letter "l" that is different between the two words. And as simple as that may sound, think about how often temptations come, and because everyone else is doing it, many Christians go along with it. Again, I am not judging, and say that with the utmost love. The world has become so desensitized over time that what would never have been considered acceptable 50 years ago now is not even questioned by most. Jesus came into the world to save sinners, of whom I was one that needed to be saved. It is by this grace and mercy that was shown to me that I seek to forever hold dear my relationship with the One who saved me.

I still remember the day I gave my life back to God. See, I was what some would call a good person. I did nice things for people. I helped others whenever and wherever I could. When I was younger, I had been to the Catholic church with my grandfather, the Baptist church with my other grandparents, and the Sunday school bus that came to our neighborhood. All those years growing up, I knew about God, but I never learned what it was to have a relationship with Him. As a kid, I heard that all sin leads to death. I was terrified because, at that age, I thought every terrible thing that happened to me resulted from lying about doing my homework.

Let us be clear; unrepented sin does open the door to the enemy in your life. But that is the beautiful thing about mercy. Jesus paid the price. All we need to do is to repent and ask for forgiveness.

When I made the decision to give my life back to God, I was committing to live for Him for the rest of my life. But as soon as the Pastor said to come down front and make it a public confession of my faith, I Immediately envisioned the Dow Jones ticker tape streaming across my forehead announcing every sin I ever committed. It stopped me in my tracks. But again, the mercy of God and His grace helped me to walk forward because the truth was, I was not confessing any sin walking down there. I was acknowledging that I made a decision for Him.

See how quickly words can change how you think about something. When I thought I had to go in front of everybody and make a confession, it terrified me. I did not want the people in the church to know what I had done wrong. That is not what Jesus is looking for. He is looking for a relationship. He wants you to come and be embraced in His perfect and unconditional love. That confession was just acknowledging that, yes, I was a sinner, but I also understood that I was forgiven.

We are not the sum of our mistakes, nor are we only defined by the accomplishments we can list. The world does not define us; we can only be defined by the One who created us.

> For He made Him who knew no sin to be sin for us, that we might become the righteousness of God in Him. 2 Corinthians 5:21

Be willing to challenge the lie.

When we do not know the truth, we will believe a lie. When you know what God's word says about you, you will see the great value He sees in you. If we look back at Romans 12:3, it warns us not to think of ourselves more highly than we ought to think. This refers to becoming prideful. The world will use phrases like "Who Do You Think You Are?" Do you think you are better than everyone else because you are a Christian? These statements lead some believers to not value Christ in them. The same is true for thinking too little of yourself.

It is not easy to see what God sees in us some days. Some days when you are going through something, it will take everything you have to see what He sees. I think that is why the verse ends with, "God has dealt to each one a measure of faith." He knew that there would be days when the only way we could see what He sees is by faith. On those tough days, make sure you are looking through the lens of faith because you can be sure someone will come along and try to cast doubt.

Ask yourself, when doubt comes, are these just feelings of doubt? Because we are not moved by our feelings. You have two parts to your brain, one is for feelings and emotions, and the other is for thinking and logic. We need to question the lie that is bringing doubt by setting aside our feelings and emotions so that we can think about it logically. As we think about it, ask yourself why this distraction, the doubt, is even coming up right now. What is on the other side of my decision if I push through this and do not allow the doubt to hinder my steps?

RECOGNIZING THE IMPACT OF IDENTITY ON YOUR LIFE

If you do not love you, then how can you love others? The truth is it is almost impossible. How can you accept love if you do not feel worthy of love? To love is to trust. You must lay down your guard and trust God, your Creator, to love you and show you who you are in Him. His perfect love will cast away your fears if you open your heart to Him. He knows the plans He has for you that are good and not evil, for you to have hope in your future and your now.

One key point I have mentioned is that God wants a relationship with you. He gave His Son that we might have life everlasting. Jesus bought our freedom so that we could be adopted as sons and daughters, His very own children, according to Galatians 4:5.

> "For you formed my inward parts; you covered me in my mother's womb. I will praise you, for I am fearfully and wonderfully made; marvelous are your works and that my soul knows very well." Psalms 139:13-14

God created you as an individual, uniquely made with a purpose. You have value, beloved! Don't believe the lie that says otherwise. Do not look to social media, Television, and the internet to try to copy someone else or to be someone you are not created to be.

In the 2003 movie "What A Girl Wants," a young girl from America is seen doing everything she can to fit into the society her father lives in. She wants a relationship with him after so many years lost to not knowing who or where he was. There is a scene where a young Ian Wallace asks Daphne Reynolds, "Why are you trying so hard to fit in when you are born to stand out?"

See, that is a picture of many of us, especially women. What experiences, trauma, or mistakes from your past have you constantly trying to fit in, trying to feel like you are enough, or seeking love in all the wrong places? Remember, you are not the sum of your mistakes, and you are not only valued by your accomplishments on a list.

In Ephesians 2:10, the Apostle Paul tells us we are God's workmanship, created in Christ Jesus for good works. Look at the creation around you; look at the birds, the sunsets, the mountains, and the valleys filled with flowers. Jesus said in Luke 12:7, "But that the very hairs of your head are all numbered. Do not fear, you are of more value than many sparrows." In Matthew 6:30, He said, "Now if God so clothes the grass of the field, which today is, and tomorrow is thrown into the oven, will He not much more clothe you, O you of little faith?"

"Greater is He that is in you than he that is in the world." 1 John 4:4

We are not in this alone. We have back-up.

"But you are a chosen generation, a royal priesthood, a holy nation, his own special people, that you may proclaim the praises of Him who called you out of darkness into His marvelous light." 1 Peter 2:9

You are Chosen. He chose you! He has called you out of the darkness of this world and into His light.

WHY THE BEST SELF-DISCOVERY AS A CHRISTIAN IS THROUGH GOD

It is critical to know who you are in Christ. As Christians, we must be led by the Spirit in all we do. Especially when we seek to understand who God is and who He created us to be. When we spend quality time reading our Bibles, we can feel His peace that surpasses understanding. The more Word that goes in, the more revelation and knowledge we get from it. Becoming connected to the Word through the Spirit helps you be sensitive to His nudging when interacting with family or coworkers.

When we read the Psalms and Proverbs regularly, we gain wisdom for everyday living in how we treat one another and how we should do our jobs. We see what it is to be so honest with God when the psalmist is angry with someone, and the Spirit in us reminds us of a situation we may have handled differently for a better outcome. The Psalmist opens his heart to the Lord in worship in a way we could never have imagined. He reveals his great sin and repents and can worship because the weight has been lifted; he is in absolute surrender. Yet instead of being taken captive, what he has been given is freedom.

As we seek to know God more, we begin to see ourselves through His Word. We start connecting with the Holy Spirit and find that we are walking in more peace and understanding. Contentment settles over us like a blanket. You begin to desire more of Him because the Living water is quenching your soul. You cannot live without it.

Let me create a picture for you. You have probably seen the giant water bucket at a waterpark that is continually filling up until it pours out over the people standing beneath it. The kids standing there are screaming with anticipation of that water being poured over them. The same can be true with the Word. You fill yourself up by reading the Word daily. The impact it is having on your heart is already life changing. Your bucket is full, and suddenly it pours out. You scream out, but not as you would expect. It is a shout of freedom; it is a shout of praise and thanksgiving. Because instead of losing what you had filled up with, that water has washed away years of heaviness you have carried around. You no longer carry the burden of shame. You are no longer weighed down by the heaviness of past sins. You feel lighter than you have ever felt before. That is living water. You find and fill yourself with that every day in the Word of God.

Bible Verses for Reflection:

- Jeremiah 1:5 - "Before I formed you in the womb I knew you, before you were born I set you apart; I appointed you as a prophet to the nations."
- Proverbs 3:5-6 - "Trust in the Lord with all your heart and lean not on your own understanding; in all your ways submit to him, and he will make your paths straight."

- Psalm 32:8 - "I will instruct you and teach you in the way you should go; I will counsel you with my loving eye on you."
- Romans 12:2 - "Do not conform to the pattern of this world, but be transformed by the renewing of your mind. Then you will be able to test and approve what God's will is—his good, pleasing, and perfect will."
- 1 Peter 2:9 But you are a chosen generation, a royal priesthood, a holy nation, his own special people, that you may proclaim the praises of Him who called you out of darkness into His marvelous light.

Before moving on, take some time to reflect on each of these verses. Allow them to frame your thinking about who you are in Christ.

Reflective Questions:

1. How has my journey of discovery with God deepened my understanding of faith and how it is a part of my identity?
2. In what ways has embracing my journey of discovery with God transformed my relationship with Him?
3. What lessons have I learned about trust, surrender, and Spirit-led guidance throughout my journey?

4. How has my journey of discovery with God influenced my perspective on purpose, meaning, and the bigger picture of life?
5. What practices or habits have I developed to nurture and sustain my connection with God during this journey of discovery?

In this chapter, we focused on our creation in the image of God and our inherent worth. It calls us to a personal relationship with God, as exemplified by Adam and Eve's fellowship with Him. It underlines the importance of grounding oneself in God's Word to avoid falling prey to deceptive influences that seek to undermine our self-perception and relationship with God. Through the story of Eve's temptation and fall, we understand why it is important to have personal knowledge and understanding of God's commands. The choices made by Adam and Eve led to consequences that shifted the course of mankind, emphasizing the power of free will and the potential harm of deception.

As we embark on a journey of self-discovery through God, we recognize the significance of renewing our minds through God's Word as opposed to conforming to worldly perspectives. The distinction made between "Word" and "World" shows how a slight deviation from God's Word could lead to worldly temptations. The essence of our identity is not by worldly standards but defined by our divine Creator.

As we immerse ourselves daily in His Word, it purifies us, stripping away years of burdens and shame. This engagement with God's Word, His living water, nourishes our souls, leading us to a life of freedom, praise, and thanksgiving. Ultimately, we need to be looking through the lens of faith, recognizing our worth and value in Christ.

In the next chapter, we will learn what it means to embrace your identity as a child of God. We will review scriptures that will help us understand how He sees His children and what His Word says about our identity in Christ.

2

KNOWING & UNDERSTANDING YOUR IDENTITY IN GOD'S EYES

"See what great love the Father has lavished on us, that we should be called children of God! And that is what we are!"

—1 JOHN 3:1

EMBRACING YOUR IDENTITY AS A BELOVED CHILD OF GOD

In society today, we do not have to look far to find someone or some personality test that proclaims it will help you better understand yourself. Social Media platforms have name tests and pick-and-choose quizzes that promise to uncover some profound information about you. The problem with these quizzes is that they are stock responses. If you do not like what it says, simply click refresh to get a new description.

For most people, our identity is found in external places and things. Where you work, who you are dating or married to, how big your house is, your reputation, the clothes you wear, and your physical appearance, to name a few. But with all these things, change is inevitable. You get older, and your body changes. If you lose your job, your lifestyle will change. One false accusation can ruin your reputation and leave you devastated.

What about your faith? If you have a relationship with God, you know that He is faithful and true. The Bible says in Hebrews 13:8, "He is the same yesterday, today, and forever." He is a firm foundation upon which you can find the truth of who He says you are. Your identity in Him is not tied to a religion. It is found in who He is and who He says you are.

Let us look at a brief list of 10 identifiers of who He is:

- Creator
- Redeemer
- Healer
- Counselor
- Comforter
- Savior
- Friend
- Strength
- Provider
- Peace

He is the all-sufficient one, everything you need and more. And because He is who He is, He holds a special place in His heart for you and me. Even the very best father you can imagine cannot compare to the Father God wants to be for us.

HOW DOES GOD SEE HIS CHILDREN

Anytime you enter a relationship with someone, whether it is a new friend or dating someone, you ask questions to find out who they are and what they like or do not like. However, most people do not come with a book describing all you want to know. It is not possible because people are changing regularly. The good news with God is He has a book, and it never changes. He even included notes and letters to let you know what He thinks of you too.

As a Father, He loves you, and chooses you, and has a purpose for your life. Here are six verses of scripture that God refers to you as His children. You are part of His family, and Romans 8:17 also tells us we are joint heirs with Christ.

Yet to all who did receive him, to those who believed in his name, he gave the right to become children of God— children born not of natural descent, nor of human decision or a husband's will, but born of God. John 1:12-13

So, in Christ Jesus, you are all children of God through faith, Galatians 3:26

Dear friends, now we are children of God, and what we will be has not yet been made known. But we know that when Christ appears, we shall be like him, for we shall see him as he is. 1 John 3:2

And, "I will be a Father to you, and you will be my sons and daughters, says the Lord Almighty." 2 Corinthians 6:18

The Spirit you received does not make you slaves, so that you live in fear again; rather, the Spirit you received brought about your adoption to sonship. And by Him, we cry, "*Abba,* Father." The Spirit himself testifies with our spirit that we are God's children. Romans 8:15-16

I will say to the north, 'Give them up!' and to the south, 'Do not hold them back.' Bring my sons from afar and my daughters from the ends of the earth—everyone who is called by my name, whom I created for my glory, whom I formed and made. Isaiah 43:6-7

As a child of God, He tells us to train up a child in the way he should go, and when He is old, he will not depart from it. Proverbs 22:6. How can He train up His children? He gave us His word. Contrary to what many people think, the Bible is not just a book of "Don'ts." It is a book filled with instructions on how to live a blessed life. When we obey our parents, we are blessed.

What the Bible Says About Identity in Christ

You have probably heard someone say, "God works in mysterious ways." But that is not how the Bible says He works. If you read through the Bible, you can recognize patterns from the Old Testament to the New Testament.

> The LORD is righteous in all his ways and faithful in
> all he does. The LORD is near to all who call on him,
> to all who call on him in truth. He fulfills the desires
> of those who fear him; he hears their cry and saves
> them. Psalms 145:17-19

He is righteous in all His ways and faithful in all He does. That does not sound mysterious to me; in fact, it is pretty clear. Let us look at a few verses to see what God's word says about your identity.

> "You are no longer foreigners and strangers, but
> fellow **citizens with God's people** and also **members
> of his household.**" Ephesians 2:19

God made him who had no sin to be sin for us, so that in him we **might become the righteousness of God**. 2 Corinthians 5:21

But you are a **chosen people, a royal priesthood**, a holy nation, **God's special possession**, that you may declare the praises of him who called you out of darkness into his wonderful light. 1 Peter 2:9 NIV

May have power, together with all the Lord's holy people, to grasp how wide and long and high and deep is the love of Christ, and to know this love that surpasses knowledge—that you may be filled to the measure of all the fullness of God. Ephesians 3:18

For we are **God's handiwork**, created in Christ Jesus to do good works, which God prepared in advance for us to do. Ephesians 2:10

*Note: Emphasis is mine to bring attention to how He sees you.

All the verses listed here point to a beautiful, strong, chosen family member. That is who you are and so much more. Take some time to do a search in the Bible on Identity in Christ. It is easiest to do if you have a Bible App on your phone or device. When I did this, it brought up over fifty verses that help you to see how God sees you.

RECOGNIZING YOUR WORTH AND VALUE IN HIM

We talked about our identity in Christ, who God is, and how He sees us. Now let us talk about your value and worth in Him. First, we need to clarify the difference between value and worth. When it comes to objects, the terms value and worth are often used interchangeably, but they can have slightly different connotations depending on the context. Both terms refer to the importance or usefulness of an object, but they can be approached from different perspectives.

Value refers to the estimated or perceived worth of an object, typically in monetary terms. It is the price or amount that someone is willing to pay or exchange for an item in a market or economic setting. For example, a rare collectible coin may have a high value because it is highly sought after by collectors, even though its intrinsic worth as a piece of metal may be relatively low.

Worth, on the other hand, encompasses a broader sense of value and extends beyond mere monetary considerations. It refers to the overall significance, usefulness, or importance of an object, often incorporating non-monetary factors such as sentimental value, emotional attachment, historical or cultural significance, or practical utility. For instance, a family heirloom passed down through generations may have significant worth due to its sentimental value and the memories associated with it, even if it holds little or no monetary value in the market.

I am so glad my value and my worth are not tied to the market, and it is not based on feelings and emotions. Our value does not come from having some position of authority or being a newbie on a job. Ephesians 2:10 said, we were God's handiwork, in Christ Jesus to do good works. In Mark 10:45, Jesus said, "For even the Son of man did not come to be served, but to serve, and to give his life as a ransom for many.

Jesus came to serve, not to be served. He was not concerned with the title or position. That is not where His value or worth came from. His value came in His identity as the Son of God. And as the Son of God, He gave His life as a ransom for us. We know we are valuable to God because He paid the price for us with the life of His Son.

What Is My Worth to God?

Through the eyes of faith, you are immeasurably precious and valuable to God. You are a unique creation, intricately woven together by Divine hands. Your worth to God is not determined by worldly standards or achievements but by the depth of love and grace bestowed upon you by God.

God's love for you is unconditional and unwavering. It transcends your flaws, mistakes, and shortcomings. You are a cherished child of God, intimately known and deeply loved. Your worth lies in the very fact that you are created in the image of God, reflecting divine qualities and potential.

God has a purpose for your life. You are not here by accident but by divine design. Your unique gifts, talents, and experiences are meant to bring about goodness, justice, and love in the world.

Whatever you may have gone through, God's grace is available to you. You are worthy of forgiveness, redemption, and transformation. God desires to see you grow, heal, and become the best version of yourself.

In the eyes of God, you are irreplaceable and valued beyond measure. Your worth is not based on external validations but on the divine love that encompasses you. Embrace your worth, embrace your identity as a beloved child of God, and live your life knowing that you are deeply valued in the eyes of the Almighty.

DISCOVERING YOUR PURPOSE AND CALLING IN GOD'S KINGDOM

It is not uncommon to question how God could use you to fulfill His purpose and plans. I am an earthly being with flaws and mistakes in my past, and I do not see how I could do anything important for God. But even with the worst past, God still redeems His children when they cry out to Him.

"To console those who mourn in Zion, to give them beauty for ashes, the oil of joy for mourning, the garment of praise for the spirit of heaviness; that

they may be called trees of righteousness, the
planting of the Lord, that he may be glorified." Isaiah
61:3

Ask God to show you what He would have you do to be the hands and feet of Jesus. You may have a testimony that you share with someone because you can relate to what they are going through. When you share how God helped you overcome and get the victory, you will encourage them. It is encouraging because, as Peter shared in Acts 10:34, "In truth, I perceive that God shows no partiality." That means that if God did it for you, He could do it for them.

The last thing Jesus said to the disciples was to go and make disciples of all nations. Does that mean you need to leave everything behind and travel the world preaching the Gospel? No, not unless God told you to do it. You would know if that is what you were called to do. There are other ways to Go into the World and make disciples. You may be a part of a serve team at church ministering to the children in Sunday School. Maybe there is a mission trip that you can't go on at this time, but you can pray for the team or even sow a financial seed to help someone else who is going. You can share what God is doing in your life with others who might be encouraged by hearing it. Anytime you do anything pointing them to God, you share His good news.

Some Guidelines From God's Word

One thing to remember is that you are not alone. Proverbs 3:6 tells us to lean not on our own understanding but to acknowledge Him, and He will make your path straight. When you spend time in the Word, you are filling your tank. You read the passages of guidance and become familiar with it, and when a situation comes up, the verses you read will guide you in how you should respond. It's like taking daily vitamins to keep your immune system strong and your joints healthy. It works as a progression and builds upon itself.

Jesus spent time discussing the Scriptures when he was a kid (see Luke 2:46-47). When Satan came to tempt Him before He began His ministry, He responded with the Word of God to shut him down (see Matthew 4:1-11).

Many of the Proverbs also point you to wise counsel. We need to make sure we are connected to the Body of Christ. We do not need to follow everyone's advice but follow Jesus's example in how He had the 12 disciples with whom He traveled and ministered. He also had a few disciples that were even closer to Him who had the opportunity to witness and be a part of significant moments in Jesus's life and ministry. Ensure the people you surround yourself with are not just saying what they think you want to hear.

"Likewise, you younger people, submit yourself to your elders. Yes, all of you be submissive to one another, and be clothed with humility, for God resists the proud but gives grace to the humble." 1 Peter 5:5

When we submit ourselves to one another and remain humble, God can grow us and help us bear fruit in our lives. Also, remember that people are sometimes led by their own ideas, so always pray and check what they have told you with what God's Word says.

"But let patience have its perfect work, that you may be perfect and complete, lacking nothing. If any of you lacks wisdom, let him ask of God, who gives to all liberally and without reproach, and it will be given to him." James 1:4-5

Do not rush into any decision without first praying and asking God for the wisdom you need to make that decision. He is faithful to give you the wisdom and understanding that you need.

I remember one occasion when it was late in the evening, and I was dealing with a sink that was clogged. I had been in my home for about 2 years, and it was just me. It was my guest bathroom that no one was using. At the time, I did not really have the money to call an emergency plumber to come out and fix my sink. I prayed, and I prayed for wisdom to know how to fix this or that God would send someone who could help me without it costing too much. After praying, I walked into the bathroom and sat on the floor, and suddenly, I recognized under the sink where I could turn the fittings at the two ends of the P trap. I grabbed a bucket and started turning those fittings. The Trap dropped, and the water drained. Then, I found the insulation from the attic that had dropped down through a drainpipe from my air condition unit in the attic.

I did not get an audible answer from God in this situation, but He led me by helping me to see what needed to be done. He gave me the wisdom I was asking for in prayer. When we spend time with Him, in His word and in prayer, we can be led to do what needs to be done in every situation.

Walking in God's Promises for Your Life

The other day my son asked me, "How do you know what God's promises are?" My answer was, "Simple, read your Bible, and you will find hundreds of promises." I know that thought can feel overwhelming, so I introduced him to these four simple promises found in the scriptures.

"No man shall be able to stand before you all the days of your life; as I was with Moses, so I will be with you. I will not leave you nor forsake you." Joshua 1:5

"Draw near to God, and He will draw near to you"
James 4:8

"Delight yourself also in the Lord, and he shall give
you the desires of your heart" Psalms 37:4

"But seek first the kingdom of God and His righteousness, and all these things shall be added to you."
Matthew 6:33

The verse Matthew 6:33 was one of the first verses I
committed to memory when I committed to living for God
for the rest of my life. I can say with all confidence that God
has honored this promise. I am not perfect at always
seeking God in all that I do, but He has been so faithful and
patient with me. When we make Him our priority, He
makes a way where there seems no other way.

How-to walk-in God's promises and wait for them

God said He has plans for you in Jeremiah 29:11. That verse
has always given me hope, peace, and joy. One day as I
continued reading, I noticed that verses 12 and 13 were
extending another promise to me. If I call upon the Lord
and pray, He will listen. If I seek Him, I will find Him.

"Then you will call upon Me and go and pray to Me, and I will listen to you. And you will seek Me and find Me, when you search for Me with all your heart." Jeremiah 29:12-13

When we pray and seek God, He hears us. But what do you do when you do not see the answers to your prayers? You wait for Him. As I said before, you do not rush to act or make a decision. Sometimes the waiting can be really hard, and you can begin to doubt. But this is when you need to pause and seek God on what He is trying to do in this season of waiting.

When the Israelites were rescued from Egypt and traveled to the promised land. They did not make it in a week, a month, or even a year. It took 40 years for them to reach the promised land. Sadly, many of them did not make it to the promised land. God needed many of them to change their hearts. After all that God rescued them from, many continue to complain and grumble about the blessings that he had given them. They could not wait for Moses to return so they had an idol made to worship. It cost them everything because they could not keep their focus on God and trust the process as He led them to the promised land.

When I prayed for a family, it was 7 years before I could see what God was doing to bring it to pass. When I recognized that I would have children through adoption and that they would be siblings, I thought I knew how that would happen. Another 7 years passed before the door was finally opened, and I opened my home as a foster parent. After a year of loving my children and being ready to let them go, I was granted the gift of adoption and I was able to keep the children that were entrusted to my care. We have been a family for 7 years now.

God was in the details. I wanted to be the best possible parent from day one. If I had children in the beginning, our life would not be what it is today. I had some healing to do, as well as changing some selfish motivations. I needed to know who I was in Christ before I could raise children to live for God. It was important that I could be whole in Christ before trying to raise kids. If I did not wait, I would not have His best. I give all thanks and glory to God for what He did in me through the process. It was absolutely worth waiting for.

When we focus our eyes on God as we wait on Him, we position ourselves to be submitted to the work He is doing in and through us. In that place of surrender, there is fullness of grace and mercy. In surrendering to Him, there is freedom and liberty. You are entering His presence.

Living Out Your Identity in Daily Life and in Him

You surrendered your life to God, and now you want to know how to live this life in Christ to the fullest. His Word will help you when you remember when the doubts come and the enemy tries to torment you with negative thoughts, you are a new creation, and you can take every thought captive under the obedience of Christ.

"Therefore, if anyone is in Christ, he is a new creation; old things have passed away; behold, all things have become new." 2 Corinthians 5:17

'We demolish arguments and every pretension that sets itself up against the knowledge of God, and we take captive every thought to make it obedient to Christ.' 2 Corinthians 10:5 NIV

Living out your identity in daily life and in Christ means aligning your actions, beliefs, and values with who you truly are and with the teachings and examples of Jesus Christ. It involves living a life of authenticity, integrity, and purpose, embracing your unique qualities and gifts, and expressing them in all areas of your life. In Christ, you find your true identity as a beloved child of God, forgiven and Redeemed by His grace.

It means reflecting His love, compassion, and humility in your relationships, seeking justice and mercy, and being a source of hope and encouragement to others. It is a journey of growth and transformation, allowing the Holy Spirit to shape you into the person God created you to be. By living out your identity in Christ, you become a living testimony of God's love and a vessel for his purposes in the world.

Bible Verses for Reflection:

- Psalm 139:16 - "Your eyes saw my unformed body; all the days ordained for me were written in your book before one of them came to be."
- Ephesians 2:10 - "For we are God's handiwork, created in Christ Jesus to do good works, which God prepared in advance for us to do."
- 2 Corinthians 5:17 - "Therefore, if anyone is in Christ, the new creation has come: The old has gone, the new is here!"
- Romans 8:17 - "Now if we are children, then we are heirs—heirs of God and co-heirs with Christ, if indeed we share in his sufferings in order that we may also share in his glory."
- 1 Peter 2:9 NIV - "But you are a chosen people, a royal priesthood, a holy nation, God's special possession, that you may declare the praises of him who called you out of darkness into his wonderful light."
- Colossians 3:10 - "and have put on the new self, which is being renewed in knowledge in the image of its Creator."
- Galatians 2:20 - "I have been crucified with Christ and I no longer live, but Christ lives in me. The life I now live in the body, I live by faith in the Son of God, who loved me and gave himself for me."

Reflective Questions:

1. How does my understanding of my identity in God's eyes differ from the worldly standards and expectations that surround me?
2. In what ways have I allowed the opinions and judgments of others to shape my perception of myself, and how can I align my identity with God's perspective instead?
3. What are the specific qualities and characteristics about myself that I believe reflect God's image within me, and how can I nurture and express them more fully?
4. How does knowing and understanding my identity in God's eyes impact the way I view and treat others, as well as how I engage with the world around me?
5. What steps can I take to deepen my relationship with God and continually seek His guidance in understanding and embracing my identity in Him?

Embracing your identity as a beloved child of God encourages us to find our self-understanding in our relationship with God, our Creator, and Redeemer, rather than fleeting external factors. We are part of God's family and His plans, which helps us understand the importance of His word as a guide for a fulfilling life. In embracing our identity in Christ, we are reminded of the numerous scriptural assurances of our worth in God's eyes, dispelling the need for worldly validation.

We need to recognize our worth and value in Him as Christians from God's perspective. It accentuates that our significance and worth are rooted in our creation in the image of God and the unique roles we are meant to fulfill in His Kingdom. It encourages us to seek God's guidance in discerning our purpose, assuring us of our preciousness to Him regardless of our human imperfections.

When we walk in God's promises for our lives, it helps us identify and rely on God's Word and the need for patience in awaiting their manifestation. God's perfect timing often serves as transformative periods of preparation for His blessings.

In the next chapter, we are going to discover how to embrace God's grace and let go of the past. From understanding the power of God's grace to releasing regret and guilt to God that holds us back. We will also touch on healing from past hurts and trauma that have held us captive.

3

EMBRACING GOD'S GRACE TO LET GO OF THE PAST

> *"But he said to me, 'My grace is sufficient for you, for my power is made perfect in weakness.' Therefore, I will boast all the more gladly about my weaknesses so that Christ's power may rest on me."*

— 2 CORINTHIANS 12:9

UNDERSTANDING THE POWER OF GOD'S GRACE

I remember the first time I truly got revelation and understanding of what God meant when he said, "My grace is sufficient, for my power is made perfect in weakness." It was the day I met my children. They were all three under three years old. I was all by myself at home with them. The first few hours went great. I had one potty training, and he accidentally locked the bathroom door. The next time he had to go, I had to walk him up the stairs to another bathroom as I carried the 1-year-old and 3-month-old. On every trip up and down, I had to carry two children. As a single first-time mom, I started to question my judgment in the decisions I made. This verse kept running through my mind. By evening my neighbor was able to come over and get the door unlocked for us.

The first days were really hard, and I will not deny it. But God met me right where I was and strengthened me. God's grace gave me the power to push through those hard days. He equipped me through His word to love them as He loved them. And His anointing and compassion helped me to walk them through a difficult time. Remember I said earlier that if God has called you to do something, you would know it. This is how I know. When He called me to adoption, He prepared me through the years of mission trips to love freely even if my heart breaks through it. Every time I had to say goodbye to the children in Guatemala, my heart was breaking. I had to learn how to say goodbye and trust that God was going to heal my heart every time. I had to trust Him that He was guiding me to the place He wanted me.

When I came home from my last mission trip, something was different in me. It was then that He showed me how I could love His children here too. I signed the papers to start the process of becoming a foster parent, and the rest is His story! I cannot take credit for the wonderful He has done in my life. Only that I had the heart to obey Him. To go where He wanted me to go and to do what He wanted me to do.

Moses, Gideon, and David experienced the grace of God and His power at a time they thought they would never make it. Moses had to stand up to Pharaoh before he led the Israelites out of Egypt. And it did not stop there; the Egyptians chased them all the way to the Red Sea. And when it looked like they were going to be overtaken, God did what only He could do and parts the Red Sea and allowed the Israelites to cross on dry ground. When the Egyptians followed them into the sea, they were swallowed up by the sea.

In Judges chapter 6, we learn about Gideon. And the angel of the Lord came to him and said, "The Lord is with you, you mighty man of valor." (Judges 6:12) Then the angel told him, "Go in this might of yours, and you shall save Israel from the hand of the Midianites" (Judges 6:14). Gideon's response to the angel of the Lord was, "My Lord, how can I save Israel? Indeed, my clan is the weakest in Manasseh, and I am the least in my father's house." (Judges 6:15) but the Lord said, "Surely I will be with you, and you shall defeat the Midianites as one man." (Judges 6:16)

Gideon called together an army to go to battle. God did not want Gideon to go to battle with the over 30,000 men that came together. He told Gideon to send home anyone who is fearful or afraid, and when he did, 22,000 men turned and went home. There were only 10,000 remaining. The Lord said there were still too many, so he gave them a test, and based on how they drank the water from the river, only 300 remained. With only 300 men, the Lord used Gideon to defeat the Midianite army.

David, a shepherd boy armed with only a slingshot and some stones, defeated the sword-bearing giant Goliath. The whole army of Israel was afraid to go out to fight the Philistine army with their giant warrior Goliath. Now David, a young man after the heart of God, heard what Goliath was saying about the army and their God. With confidence in what the Lord had done in his life, he went forward and told the king, the Lord who delivered me from the paw of the lion and from the paw of the bear, He will deliver me from the hand of this Philistine.

David's confidence was not in his own strength. His confidence was in the Lord, his deliverer. David went out against Goliath with only a slingshot and a few stones. He ran towards the giant and threw a single stone and defeated Goliath. All glory was given to God in his victory.

When you are going through something, remember you are not alone. If you cry out to God, He will hear. When you seek Him for the wisdom to get through and make the right decisions, He is faithful to guide you.

We must understand when things seem the darkest, when we are at the end of ourselves; it is only in God that we find hope. He has given us free will and the right to make choices for ourselves. Sometimes those choices that we make are wrong. They are not the best way that we should go. But by His grace, He will help us get back on the right track when we ask Him. Our choices could lead us to go through some things that are hard and uncomfortable, like there is no way out.

Grace is God's unmerited favor. Looking at God's word is the best way to understand the fullness of His grace.

"For by grace you have been saved through faith, and that not of yourselves; it is the gift of God." Ephesians 2:8

"Let us, therefore, come boldly to the throne of grace, that we may obtain mercy and find Grace to help us in time of need." Hebrews 4:16

"And the Word became flesh and dwelt among us, and we beheld his glory, the glory of the only begotten of the father, full of grace and truth." John 1:14

"For sin shall not have dominion over you, for you are not under the law but under grace." Romans 6:14

"But he gives more grace. Therefore, he says: God resists the proud, but gives grace to the humble." James 4:6

RELEASING REGRETS AND GUILT TO GOD

Moving past regret is important if we want to see a change in our lives. We have all been in situations where we have said things, we wish we had not or done things we should not. Mistakes, bad habits, or not following through with a commitment to ourselves can cause regret. So, what is regret? It is a feeling of sorrow or remorse over something you did, over something you said, or something you should have done but did not.

What makes you feel regretful? A softened heart for God is what will make you feel regretful. It is your conscience's awareness of right and wrong.

"For godly sorrow produces repentance leading to salvation, not to be regretted." 2 Corinthians 7:10

"Or do you despise the riches of his goodness, forbearance, and long-suffering, not knowing that the goodness of God leads you to repentance?"
Romans 2:4

The goodness of God leads you to repentance which leads you to salvation. Salvation is in Christ Jesus, which leads to healing and wholeness in Him. Through repentance, we have forgiveness, and we no longer have to carry the heaviness of regret. We walk in freedom and grace, joy, and hope.

Getting Past Guilt: Overcoming Barriers to Feeling Forgiven

Take some time and think over the last year and any regrets you may have. Give yourself permission to think and be honest with yourself about how those regrets have made you feel. Envision yourself taking the burden of each of these regrets and laying them at the foot of the cross as you ask God to forgive you. Give them to God and ask Him in return to show you how to use them for His glory. I know it may seem strange that your past regrets could be used for His glory, but you never know how the testimony of redemption can be used to change someone's heart. Now as you move forward, remember you are forgiven.

"If we confess our sins, he is faithful and just to forgive us our sins and to cleanse us from all unright-eousness first." 1 John 1:9

"There is therefore now no condemnation to those who are in Christ Jesus." Romans 8:1

Look at some examples from the Bible of men who, even though they had great reasons for regrets, did not get stuck in the regrets. As they repented and asked God to forgive them they were able to move on and be mightily used by God.

Moses killed an Egyptian and hid the body, and when somebody brought it up the next day, he fled. God still used Moses to deliver the Israelites out of Egypt.

David took another man's wife and then had him killed in battle.

Paul, who was formerly known as Saul, was persecuting, and killing Christians until he had a face-to-face with Jesus. When his eyes were opened, and he believed in Jesus, he went on to minister the gospel to the Gentiles.

Remember these words from Paul from Philippians 3 when you feel stuck dwelling on your past regrets.

> "Not that I have already attained, or I am already perfected; but I press on, that I may lay hold of that for which Christ Jesus has also laid hold of me. Brethren, I do not count myself to have apprehended; but one thing I do, forgetting those things which are behind and reaching forward to those things which are ahead, I pressed towards the goal for the prize of the upward call of God in Christ Jesus." Philippians 3:12-14

We cannot rewrite history. We cannot change the past.

I will list a few lies the enemy will tell you as you try to move forward. This is what he held me back with, trying to keep me from walking in the fullness of God's grace and mercy. Yes, my sin was deserving of death, but Christ paid the price for me so that I could be forgiven and have an eternal relationship with the Father.

Lie #1 My sin was too great! God could never forgive me for that.

Lie #2 I have not been punished enough for what I did. I should suffer because of what I did to someone else.

Lie #3 Maybe God has forgiven me, but how can I forgive myself?

Lie #4 God must not be finished punishing me because I am still suffering as a consequence of my sin.

Lie #5 How can I forgive God when so much has happened to me in my life?

Dear one, you are not alone. So many Christians today have suffered through things done to them or suffered from the guilt of things they have done to others. The enemy wants to keep you bound up in these lies so that you cannot walk forward into the forgiveness, grace, and mercy that God has for you. With forgiveness comes freedom. God has forgiven you. He already paid the price with the life of His Son.

HEALING FROM PAST WOUNDS AND TRAUMA

Joseph was sold into slavery by his brothers so they could get rid of him. But what the enemy meant for evil, God used for good. Joseph had already received visions from the Lord through dreams. And even though he did not understand them, the hardship of being sold into slavery was still very real. He had every reason to be angry at his brothers. But as you read Joseph's story, God's favor and grace were on Joseph.

Even though he was a slave, he was put in charge of the other slaves, and God prospered him in everything that he did in Potiphar's house. The enemy came again to tear Joseph down and caused him to be thrown in jail for something he did not do. God was with him still, and in jail, he found favor with the guards. After a time, he met the person who could go before the pharaoh and tell him about him. He became second in command under Pharaoh. This brought forth the deliverance for the Israelites from a famine that was soon to come.

In the Bible, there are two scriptures that are foundational to a biblical understanding of trauma. Both were written by David. If you look at the life of David, he could easily be considered one of the most traumatized people in the Bible besides Jesus. He was constantly being attacked by others with a jealous spirit. He was being attacked for his belief in God. Let us look at these two verses and how David describes his trust in God for healing and deliverance from a broken heart.

"The Lord is near to those who have a broken heart and saves such as have a contrite spirit. Many are the afflictions of the righteous, but the Lord delivers him out of them all." Psalms 34:18-19

"He heals the brokenhearted and binds up their wounds." Psalms 147:3

This promise that He will heal your broken heart is a promise to make you whole again. I imagine The Potter sitting at his wheel and wetting the pieces of broken clay and putting the pieces back together again. Only this time, it becomes stronger as He wets the clay with His tears. He lends a part of Himself to the vessel He repairs, giving it the strength, it did not have before. The vessel now becomes a vessel of honor that can be used by Him as it becomes a reflection of Him.

Identifying emotional wounds in ourselves is vital if we are to go to our Great Physician. Need to identify the symptoms and recognize them for what they are, a symptom. When we do not deal with the symptoms, we cannot find true healing. If you cut your arm and do not take care of it, the bleeding may stop, but if you do not put on the ointment and the bandage, how are you going to keep it from getting infected?

The same is true with emotional wounds. If you do not take them to God, they become an infection inside of you, bringing forth the symptoms that we are about to cover.

- Bitterness
- Unforgiveness
- Overly sensitive over things from the past
- Emotional outbursts of anger and rage
- Feeling unloved
- Irritability
- Escapism

To find true healing for these inner wounds or past traumas, we first must be honest with ourselves and how we have suppressed these things. We know that there is a wound that we want to be healed from, but sometimes we are afraid to look at the past for how hurt we may feel in the process. Is there someone in your past that hurt you, physically or emotionally? Recognizing this is the first step to healing. What are the things that you have not let go of that are leaving you feeling wounded or causing you to hold on to unforgiveness in your heart? Do not make excuses for what they have done. Being honest about what was done and how it made you feel is very important.

It is so important that you get to the root and the specific reasons why these wounds have not healed. Much like a physical wound can get infected, your emotional wounds can get infected if they are not brought into the light.

Bacteria and infections grow in dark places. Bringing them into the light of Jesus is the only way to find true healing.

The foundational key to inner healing is to know that God loves you and he has already forgiven you. He is standing there with open arms accepting you as you are. He accepts you as you are, yet he will not leave you as you are because he wants you healed and whole in Jesus.

The keys to inner healing come with your understanding of God and how he feels about you and your healing.

- God Loves You
- God Forgives You
- God is not angry or disappointed in you.
- God is the source of your healing.
- God is the source of your deliverance.

"Surely, he has borne our griefs and carried our sorrows; yet we esteemed him stricken, smitten by God, and afflicted. But He was wounded for our transgressions, He was bruised for our iniquities; the chastisement for our peace was upon Him, and by His stripes, we are healed." Isaiah 53:4-5

Allow God to heal the hidden wounds. Allow yourself to be open with God. For we are His workmanship, created in Christ Jesus for good works. Through forgiveness of our sins, we become new creations. Allow Him to create something new in you as you release the burdens you were never meant to carry.

Bible Verses for Reflection:

- Isaiah 43:18-19 - "Forget the former things; do not dwell on the past. See, I am doing a new thing! Now it springs up; do you not perceive it? I am making a way in the wilderness and streams in the wasteland."
- Psalm 103:12 - "As far as the east is from the west, so far has he removed our transgressions from us."
- Philippians 3:13-14 - "Brothers and sisters, I do not consider myself yet to have taken hold of it. But one thing I do: Forgetting what is behind and straining toward what is ahead, I press on toward the goal to win the prize for which God has called me heavenward in Christ Jesus."
- Matthew 6:14-15 - "For if you forgive other people when they sin against you, your heavenly Father will also forgive you. But if you do not forgive others their sins, your Father will not forgive your sins."

Reflective Questions:

1. What past experiences or mistakes am I finding it challenging to let go of and fully embrace God's grace for?

2. How has holding onto the weight of my past hindered my growth, joy, and ability to experience the fullness of God's grace in my life?

3. What fears or beliefs might be keeping me from fully accepting and embracing God's forgiveness and redemption for my past?

4. In what ways can I actively practice self-compassion and extend the same grace to myself that God offers, allowing me to heal and move forward?

5. What practical steps can I take to surrender my past to God, release any burdens or shame, and embrace His grace to live fully in the present and future He has for me?

When we begin to understand the power of God's grace, we recognize the profound, supportive, and fortifying nature of God's grace, especially during periods of hardship or personal adversity. God's grace is a powerful tool we can lean to during challenging times, providing strength when we feel weak or overwhelmed.

Getting past guilt is necessary to overcome barriers to feeling forgiven. When we practice giving our regrets to God and asking for His forgiveness, it leads to freedom from condemnation.

To heal from past wounds and trauma, we must identify and confront emotional wounds, including bitterness, unforgiveness, and feelings of being unloved. These wounds are symptoms of unhealed inner trauma. Understanding

God's love, forgiveness, and His role as the source of healing and deliverance is crucial for inner healing.

As we move into the next chapter, our focus will be on forgiveness. Learning why it is so important to let go of grudges and offenses toward others. Understanding the power of God's forgiveness and extending it to others.

4

LEARNING TO FORGIVE AS YOU HAVE BEEN FORGIVEN

"Bear with each other and forgive one another if any of you has a grievance against someone. Forgive as the Lord forgave you."

— COLOSSIANS 3:13

THE TRANSFORMATIVE POWER OF FORGIVENESS

What is forgiveness? It is letting go of the anger or resentment that you are holding onto because of what someone did that hurt you. It is taking back control from the person that hurt you. True forgiveness can, in fact, invoke profound emotions of understanding and compassion towards the one who inflicted the pain.

It is important to note that it does not entail forgetting or justifying the wrongdoing committed against you. Furthermore, forgiveness does not always require reconciling with the individual responsible for the harm. Rather, it bestows a unique sense of peace that enables you to redirect your focus toward your own personal growth and resilience, empowering you to continue your journey in life.

Some of the benefits of forgiving someone begin with peace of mind. When you let it go and let God help you, He gives you His peace that passes understanding. As you begin to walk in that peace, your health can improve in the areas of your immune system and blood pressure. Your mental health begins to improve by reducing anxiety, stress, and depression.

Let us look at some scriptures on forgiveness:

> "For if you forgive men their trespasses, your heavenly Father will also forgive you. But if you do not forgive men their trespasses, neither will your Father forgive your trespasses." Matthew 6:14-15

> "Let all bitterness, wrath, anger, clamor, and evil speaking be put away from you, with all malice. And be kind to one another, tenderhearted, forgiving one another, even as God in Christ forgave you."
> Ephesians 4:31-32

Even as Christ forgave you. If we do not forgive others, God cannot forgive us.

One thing I have found to be true about forgiveness is that once I make the choice to forgive, I also must make the choice to stop talking about it. Look at Ephesians 4:31 again, "Let all bitterness, wrath, anger, clamor, and evil speaking be put away from you.

If you go back a few verses in Ephesians 4 and look at verses 29 and 30 it puts these verses into context.

> "Let no corrupt word proceed out of your mouth, but what is good for necessary edification, that it may impart grace to the hearers. And do not grieve the Holy Spirit of God, by whom you were sealed for the day of redemption." Ephesians 4:29-30

See, when you make the choice to forgive someone, you must stop talking about it. You must not be speaking ill of them. Like I said earlier, you do not have to be friends; you do not have to make up and try to reconcile, but you do have to forgive. The enemy will use your words if you start talking about them to stir up your anger and resentment again and again and again. A part of that hurt may be with you for the rest of your life, but with time and with God's grace, you will be able to walk out of victory to where it is just a memory that you have overcome.

Why is it so easy to hold a grudge?

Holding a grudge is often an easy path due to several factors. Firstly, human nature tends to amplify negative experiences because that is what the enemy wants you to do. Fear of vulnerability and potential future harm also contribute, as holding a grudge may serve as a protective mechanism. It requires effort, empathy, and self-reflection to overcome these tendencies and choose forgiveness which often demands letting go of pride, embracing vulnerability, and seeking personal growth.

What are the effects of holding a grudge?

If you are having a hard time letting go and forgiving someone, think about the weight of it being like a suitcase filled with all the offense and hurt from the situation. Some people might call it extra baggage. When you do not let go of the hurt and forgive, you choose to carry that suitcase around with you everywhere you go. You carry it into new relationships. You might carry it into your workplace. You might carry it on vacation with you. It is all right there with you waiting to be unpacked and felt all over. Is that what you really want? To hold on to it and carry it with you throughout the rest of your life.

Now imagine having to hold that suitcase up off the floor for a whole hour. Probably after 30 minutes, you would have already switched hands a few times and felt like that suitcase was getting heavier by the minute. When we chose to forgive, we let go of that suitcase. We are laying it down at the foot of the cross and saying Lord, as you have forgiven me, I choose to forgive this person. Help me to leave this bag and not pick it up again.

> "Come to me, all you who labor and are heavy laden, and I will give you rest. take my yoke upon you and learn from me, for I am gentle and lowly in heart, and you will find rest for your souls. For my yoke is easy, and my burden is light." Matthew 11:28-30

Do you think Jesus might be calling out to you in Matthew 11:28-30? Has the weight of the burden of unforgiveness made you heavy laden? Would you like to find rest? He is here for you. Forgive and begin to rest in Him.

How do I move toward a state of forgiveness?

Moving towards a state of forgiveness involves several key principles. First, it is essential to acknowledge one's own need for forgiveness and recognize the extent of God's forgiveness toward us. This understanding helps cultivate a humble and compassionate heart. Prayer plays a crucial role in seeking God's guidance and strength in extending forgiveness. Meditating on God's word, particularly teachings on forgiveness and love, can also transform our mindset. Additionally, forgiveness requires letting go of bitterness and replacing it with kindness and tenderheartedness. Finally, imitating Jesus Christ, who forgave his enemies, those who crucified Him, serves as a powerful example to our own journey toward forgiveness.

What happens if I cannot forgive someone?

Forgiving someone who has not asked for forgiveness can be very difficult. But just as Jesus forgave all of mankind as He was nailed on the cross, we must make a choice like he did to forgive. Because in forgiving them, we can be forgiven. If you find it difficult to forgive someone, take some time to think about situations when you have been forgiven. Consider for a moment there may have been outside influences that caused the person to react the way they did. This is not an excuse for them treating you wrong. Ask yourself how you would have responded if you were in their place.

Forgiveness is a process that we must walk out. When we choose to release it to God, we must do our best to walk in love with them. I remember one time I was dealing with a lot of hurt in my heart over the way someone was treating me. I had felt rejected and unloved. When I took time to pray about it and really seek God on what I needed to do, He helped me to understand I needed to forgive them, love them, and pray for them. I did not have to walk in a close relationship with them. The beautiful thing in this testimony is that God did help bring restoration to that relationship. When we put it in God's hands, He knows how to handle it the right way. I had been ready to give up, but He knew the value in the restoration. He knows because of the price He paid in giving His own Son for us to be restored to Him.

What if the person I am forgiving does not change?

The other person changing is not the point. You can pray all day long for another person to change, and you will never see anything happen. When you get out of the mindset that they need to change and begin praying FOR them, not ABOUT them, God can do a work in you and in them.

Even though I am not married yet, I bought the book by Stormie Omartian, "The Power of a Praying Wife." I found it interesting that her first chapter was about praying for your husband's wife. You read that right. As I read through it, she addresses how you will not see change in someone else if you are not first willing to check your own heart attitude. You must give it all to God, the hurt, the anger, the resentment, in all honesty. Only then will you see the change you are looking for.

When you give it all to God and are willing to ask God to help you with your own heart, He can do a work between you. This applies to all people you may have been hurt or offended by. Ask God to help heal your heart so you can pray for them with the right attitude. Pray for you to have the right heart attitude to pray for them even if you do not desire a relationship with them.

What if I am the one who needs forgiveness?

Remember, just as you must go through a process to forgive someone else, the person you may have harmed will need to do the same. Take time to be honest with yourself about the situation. Don't judge yourself too hard, and when you reach out to ask them for forgiveness, be sincere. Allow them to see that you are truly sorry, and don't make excuses. Help them to see you are taking responsibility for your actions. If they do not receive your apology well, give them time and pray that God will heal their heart and mind and remove any offense.

UNDERSTANDING GOD'S FORGIVENESS AND EXTENDING IT TO OTHERS

As we begin to fully understand the depth of the forgiveness we are given in Christ, we must learn to extend the same forgiveness to others. In 2 Timothy 2:1, Paul's letter to Timothy starts with, "You therefore, my son, be strong in the grace that is in Christ Jesus." He is telling Timothy to be strong in grace just as Christ was strong in grace towards others. In verse 3, Paul goes on to say, "You, therefore, must endure hardship as a good soldier of Jesus Christ."

Any good soldier knows you follow your leader into battle. Jesus is our leader, but we are not battling people, it is a spiritual battle that we are dealing with. I am reminded of my children when they get in trouble or think they are in trouble, they tell me "I didn't mean to do it. I'm sorry, just give me another chance and I will do better." What they are asking for is grace. They made a mistake and did something that might upset me. At that moment, I could stay mad about it, or I could show grace, forgive them, and move on.

There is an acrostic that I love about Grace, God's riches at Christ's expense. When you look at grace from that perspective, remembering all that Christ endured for you, how can we now extend the same grace to others? Our Salvation was paid for at the cross. It was for the forgiveness of our sins. We did not earn it. It is a gift from God.

If God has forgiven you of every single sin, you have ever committed, and I do mean every sin, what are you holding onto against someone else? Bitterness and resentment must be dealt with. You do not want to hang on to them. Are you bitter with your parents for how they raised you? Thinking they did not love you enough, they did not care enough, or they were not this or that other thing you feel you are missing. Let me say now, I do not make light of your situation. You may have experienced abuse of some form and that is not acceptable. I am not excusing that at all. It was real and you are hopefully working on healing from that trauma. I pray you seek the right help to walk you through the process. Part of your healing will come through forgiveness.

What I will do here is ask you to consider something about your parent(s). What was their childhood like? Were their parents raising them the same way you were raised? If you look back, generationally, there is usually a pattern in parenting. Your parent's model what was modeled for them. Their parents modeled what they experienced. And so on.

I used to hold a form of judgment against my parents that I regret deeply. Some of the mistakes they made were just that, mistakes. They were not trying to ruin my life and they did not do anything out of malice towards me. They were doing their best to survive an ever-changing world. They loved like they were loved. They raised me trying to do better than their parents, just like I try to do better with my kids. They did what they knew or learned to do, and I am stronger for it.

I make mistakes with raising my kids, and I can feel like I have failed them at times. When I recognize what I have done wrong, I do my best to go back and let them know that I may not have handled something well or the right or best way, but that I do love them, and I ask them to forgive me. We must give that same grace to our parents, who did the best they could with what they had and did their best to raise us. Who at times felt like they failed us because they could not provide or be all that we needed them to be.

Consider this point in all your relationships. The other person could be going through something. They may not know better because of cultural differences. Whatever they may have done to cause your offense, bitterness, or resentment, is it utterly worth holding on to, or could you choose to forgive, because it is a choice, and allow there to be peace between you?

What Is Bitterness?

If I were to define bitterness according to the Merriam-Webster Dictionary, it is marked by intensity or severity (as of distress or hatred). Bitterness is a hard or heavy burden to carry. In the Bible, we learned part of the Passover dinner was bitter herbs. This was used to remind them of the bitterness of slavery they had been in for the last 400 years. The bitter herbs were used to remind them of how terrible things were before.

For a moment, think about what it is like when you become bitter about something that has been done to you. Every time you think about it, it leaves you feeling resentful and angry. Or, as they say, it leaves a bitter taste in your mouth. That is why bitterness is a bad taste that does not go away quickly. It lingers and distorts the taste of other things. Unfortunately, bitterness goes deeper than that. When bitterness gets rooted deep into your heart, it can affect your well-being and the way you work with other people. It does not just affect the person who harmed you; it starts to affect other people in your life.

Let us break down some key points about forgiveness:

- Forgiveness goes beyond forgetting or excusing: Forgiving someone is not about pretending that the hurtful actions never occurred or making excuses for the wrongdoings. It involves acknowledging the hurt but choosing to release the negative emotions attached to it.
- Letting go of anger, resentment, and revenge: Forgiveness involves actively working on releasing feelings of anger, resentment, and the desire for revenge towards the person who caused the harm. It is about freeing oneself from the burden of carrying these negative emotions.
- Extending love and mercy: True forgiveness involves showing compassion and extending love and mercy to the person who hurt us. It is an act of selflessness and a willingness to see humanity in others, regardless of their actions.
- Forgiving because God has forgiven us: In many teachings, forgiveness is often tied to the understanding that God has forgiven humanity for its mistakes and sins. Therefore, believers are encouraged to follow God's example and extend forgiveness to others.

Forgiveness can be a challenging and transformative process. It is a personal journey that allows individuals to heal from emotional wounds and brings growth and understanding. By choosing forgiveness, people can break the cycle of negativity and find peace within themselves and their relationships with others.

GOD'S PLAN FOR FORGIVENESS

God shows us his plan for forgiveness through His Word. Let us look at the following scriptures:

And forgive us our debts, as we also have forgiven our debtors. Matthew 6:12

Therefore, as God's chosen people, holy and dearly loved, clothe yourselves with compassion, kindness, humility, gentleness, and patience. Bear with each other and forgive one another if any of you has a grievance against someone. Forgive as the Lord forgave you. Colossians 3:12-13

Do not judge, and you will not be judged. Do not condemn, and you will not be condemned. Forgive, and you will be forgiven. Luke 6:37 NIV

Therefore, if you are offering your gift at the altar and there, remember that your brother or sister has something against you, leave your gift there in front of the altar. First go and be reconciled to them then come and offer your gift. Matthew 5:23-24 NIV

No matter what you do, take it to the word of God, pray about it, and ask God to help you to choose to forgive. Ask him to help you set up healthy boundaries if that is what is necessary. If you would like to see a restoration, ask Him to guide you in what you need to do to bring that about. But most of all, trust Him and remember you are not alone on this journey.

Thoughts to Help You Forgive Others

Some things to consider when you are having a tough time forgiving someone.

- If you had to make a top ten list of sins you have committed against God, yet He forgave you. Don't you think you could extend the same forgiveness to someone who hurt you?
- If God is telling you in Matthew 5:23-24, you are to forgive any offense before you bring any offering to the altar, just as it is important to repent if you have done something to someone else. You can only control your heart and the choices you make.
- It may seem impossible to forgive someone in your own strength. That is why God gave us the Holy Spirit. Jesus told the people in Matthew 19:26 "With men this is impossible, but with God all things are possible." He will help you.

Bible Verses for Reflection:

- Matthew 6:15 - "But if you do not forgive others their sins, your Father will not forgive your sins."
- Mark 11:25 - "And when you stand praying, if you hold anything against anyone, forgive them, so that your Father in heaven may forgive you your sins."
- Ephesians 4:32 - "Be kind and compassionate to one another, forgiving each other, just as in Christ God forgave you."
- Luke 6:37 - "Do not judge, and you will not be judged. Do not condemn, and you will not be condemned. Forgive, and you will be forgiven."

Reflective Questions:

1. In what areas of my life do I struggle the most with extending forgiveness to others, even though I have experienced God's forgiveness in my own life?
2. How does holding onto resentment and unforgiveness impact my own well-being, relationships, and spiritual growth?
3. What lessons can I learn from reflecting on the depth and magnitude of God's forgiveness toward me, and how can I apply those lessons to extend forgiveness to others?
4. Are there any misconceptions or barriers that I need to address to fully embrace and practice forgiveness as I have been forgiven by God?

5. How can I cultivate a heart of forgiveness and compassion, not only for those who have hurt me directly but also for those who may find it harder to forgive or have caused harm on a larger scale?

In this chapter, we discussed the nature of forgiveness, describing it as an act of releasing resentment or anger towards someone who has caused harm, not to forget or justify their actions, but as a tool to regain control and focus on personal growth. Forgiveness does not necessarily require reconciliation, but it does bring profound understanding, compassion, and a unique sense of peace. The benefits of forgiveness are far-reaching, impacting both physical and mental health by reducing stress, anxiety, and depression and potentially improving immune function and blood pressure. We draw on biblical scriptures to underscore the divine mandate for forgiveness, emphasizing that failing to forgive not only disrupts our relationship with God but also fuels resentment and anger.

We learned that we must let go of this weight of unforgiveness, laying it down at the foot of the cross as a means of attaining rest and relief. As we understand God's forgiveness and extend it to others, we are to model the life of Jesus, embodying strength in grace and endurance in hardships, to fight spiritual battles, including forgiving those who have wronged us. With God's help, all things are possible. Seek God's guidance in setting up healthy boundaries and work towards reconciliation when possible. You are not alone on this journey.

The love of God that passes all understanding will be discussed in the next chapter. We will learn how to break down the barriers to receiving God's unconditional love, which will allow us to love others as He loves us.

5

OPENING YOUR HEART TO GOD'S LOVE

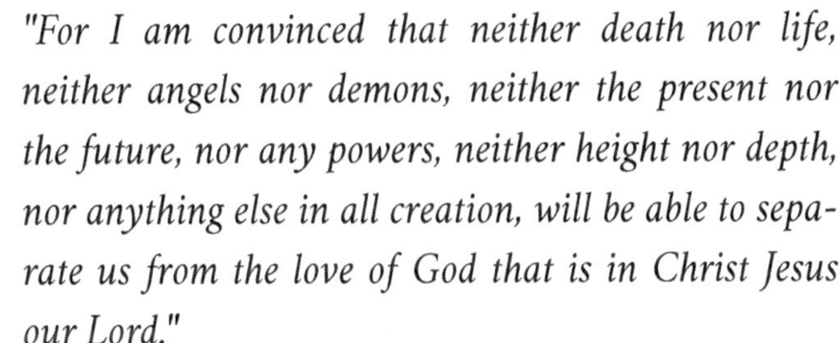

"For I am convinced that neither death nor life, neither angels nor demons, neither the present nor the future, nor any powers, neither height nor depth, nor anything else in all creation, will be able to separate us from the love of God that is in Christ Jesus our Lord."

— ROMANS 8:38-39

EXPERIENCING THE DEPTH OF GOD'S LOVE

You must experience the love of God to understand it fully. There are no limits to his love. There is no sin so great that God changes His love for you. Psalms 103:12 reminds us, "As far as the east is from the west, so far has He removed our transgressions from us." That is His gift to us,

His grace and forgiveness. It removes the sin and shame. There is no condemnation in Christ, according to Romans 8:1.

As a parent, it is a bit easier to understand this love. No matter how badly your child behaves, you still love them. Before I adopted my children, I sometimes felt as though my behavior, or my attitude would cause me to lose a measure of God's love. As if every time I did something wrong, it made God love me less. That was because I experienced conditional love from people in my life. If someone decided they did not love me anymore, they would leave, and nothing I could do would bring them back to loving me.

With my children, though, I see how the love of God passes all understanding. I could not imagine not loving them. My love for them is deeper than any love I have known, and that is only because I have experienced His great love for me. No matter what they do, I do not love them less. I do not love the unruly behavior, but I love them the same.

There is a saying, hate the sin, not the sinner. We are all sinners and have a sinful nature through Adam. However, through Christ, we have all been redeemed. Remember John 3:16-17, "For God so loved the world, He gave His only begotten Son, that whoever believes in Him should not perish but have everlasting life. For God did not send His Son into the world to condemn the world, but that the world through Him might be saved."

What Does Scripture Teach about God's Love for Us?

Let us first look at the prodigal son, as many of us can relate to leaving home and living the life we wanted to live without regard for the price our parents paid to help us grow into mature responsible adults. We had all the answers without the resources of our own. The prodigal or lost son, as mentioned in Luke 15:11-32, tells us of a son who went to his father and demanded to receive all his inheritance. The father gave him his inheritance, and he went off and squandered it away with partying and foolish living. When a severe famine came, and he had no money left, he wound up taking a job feeding the pigs. And when he was extremely hungry, he remembered that every one of his father's servants had more than enough to eat. So, he made the decision to go back and become a servant to his father. And when he was still a great way off, his father saw him and had compassion. (Author paraphrase)

It says that while he was still a great way off his father saw him. That meant his father had been watching for him to return. And his father did not make him a servant. He celebrated his son's homecoming and gave him his ring, his sandals, and a robe to mark him as a son. He got the fattened calf and threw a party. Now we will not go into what the brother had to say about it, but my point here is that the father, like God, is always watching out for us. When we walk away from Him, he is not turning his back on us as we have with Him. He is ever-present and ever watching over us. It is His great love for us that he never gives up on us.

He also wants us to love like He does. Growing into a loving person is dependent on you knowing and believing God's great love for you. How will you know or come to believe He loves you so deeply? You must spend time reading the scriptures.

> And we have known and believed the love that God has for us. God is love, and he who abides in love abides in God, and God in him. 1 John 4:16

Jesus did not just pray for the disciples, He prayed for all believers, including you and me. He prayed for all to become one with Him and the Father that we would believe God sent Him. Verse 23 goes on to say that God loves us as He loved His Son Jesus.

> I do not pray for these alone, **but also for those who will believe in me through their word** John 17:20 (added emphasis is mine)

> "That they may be made perfect in one, and that the world may know that you have sent me, and have loved them as You have loved Me. John 17:23b

> Verse 26 ends with, "that the love with which You loved Me may be in them, and I in them.

When I look at these verses, and I recognize that Jesus, the Son of God, was praying for me that I would believe through their word, I am overwhelmed with the loving kindness and patience He showed me. Jesus wanted us to experience the magnified love of the Father that He felt when He asked God "that the love with which You loved Me may be in them." I am forever thankful for His great love, not only the love He has shown me but the capacity to love as God loved Jesus, which Jesus prayed for us to have in us.

THE GREATEST DEMONSTRATION OF GOD'S LOVE FOR US

"For God so loved the world, He gave His only begotten Son, that whoever believes in Him should not perish but have everlasting life. For God did not send His Son into the world to condemn the world, but that the world through Him might be saved."
John 3:16-17

What did it cost God to show His great Love for us? It cost Him His only Son. Jesus lived as a man in this world, although He knew no sin.

"Now hope does not disappoint, because the love of God has been poured out in our hearts by the Holy Spirit who is given to us. For when we were still without strength, in due time Christ died for the ungodly. For scarcely for a righteous man will one die; yet perhaps for a good man someone would even dare to die. But God demonstrates his own love towards us, and that while we were still sinners, Christ died for us." Romans 5:5-8

While we were yet sinners, Christ chose to die for our sins so we could be returned to the Father as a joint heir with Christ.

"Behold what manner of love the Father has bestowed on us, that we should be called children of God! Therefore, the world does not know us, because it did not know Him. Beloved, now we are children of God; and it has not yet been revealed what we shall be, but we know that when He is revealed, we shall be like Him, for we shall see Him as He is. And everyone who has this hope in him purifies himself, just as He is pure." 1 John 3:1-3

When you consider the immense value of the gift of salvation, you can understand the love attached to the gift.

"Therefore, my Father loves me, because I lay down my life that I may take it again. No one takes it from me, but I lay it down of myself. I have power to lay it down, and I have power to take it up again. This command I have received from my Father. "John 10:17-18

No one took Jesus's life; He chose to lay it down for our benefit in obedience to the will of the Father.

3 Timeless Truths about God's Love for Us in His Word

1. **God's love passes all understanding** - - "to know the love of Christ which passes knowledge; that you may be filled with all the fullness of God." Ephesians 3:19 Imagine being filled with the love of God. Being able to love no matter what happens. Imagine the peace that comes with that perfect love.

2. **Nothing can separate us from the love of God -** "Who shall separate us from the love of Christ? Shall tribulation, or distress, or persecution, or famine, or nakedness, or peril, or sword? As it is written: "For your sake we are killed all day long; we are counted as sheep for the slaughter." Yet in all these things, we are more than conquerors through him who loved us. For I am persuaded that neither death nor life, nor angels nor principalities nor powers, nor things present nor things to come, nor height nor depth, nor any other created thing, shall be able to separate us from the love of God which is in Christ Jesus our Lord." Romans 8:35-39 What separated us from God, in the beginning, was sin. Now through Christ's death on the cross, the barrier has been broken. We are no longer separated. We have been restored to the Father through the Blood of the Lamb.

3. **We can experience the Love of God** - - "that Christ may dwell in your hearts through faith; that you, being rooted and grounded in love, may be able to comprehend with all the saints what is the width and length and depth and height." Ephesians 3:17-18 To be rooted and grounded in love is to be connected and live as one with the Father as Jesus was one with God.

How Does God's Love for Us Change Our Lives?

Experiencing God's love is like getting a heart transplant. The donor already gave His life for you over 2,000 years ago. When you begin to experience His love, it changes you from the inside out. It begins to change your selfish love to selfless love, and you can love others like never before. We have more compassion for others, and we can forgive more easily. You feel lighter because the burdens of the past begin to lift as you cast your cares on Him.

Embracing God's Unconditional Love and Acceptance

As you begin to embrace His love for you and walk in deeper love with others, you may feel resistance at times. This is because you have an enemy that wants you to fall, fail and lose this connection with God. But there is hope in the Word.

"Therefore, submit to God. Resist the devil, and he will flee from you. Draw near to God, and He will draw near to you." James 4:7-8

BREAKING DOWN BARRIERS TO RECEIVING GOD'S LOVE

Reasons We Struggle to Experience God's Love

What are some reasons that cause us to struggle when it comes to experiencing God's love? Most likely, the lie the enemy has been telling you throughout your life is trying to stop you now. Here are a few barriers that I recognized when I made the decision to give my life back to God. Included with each reason is the truth in the Word that proves it is a lie. You can be sure God does not stop loving you, and there is nothing you can do to change that. If you are not feeling or experiencing His love, there is a lie or barrier that has come between you.

1. We are holding unforgiveness in our hearts against someone who hurt us. "And be kind to one another, tenderhearted, forgiving one another, even as God in Christ forgave you." Ephesians 4:32
2. I don't know who I am in Christ; there must be something wrong with me because God can't love someone like me., "Behold what manner of love the

Father has bestowed on us, that we should be called children of God! 1 John 3:1a

3. Because of certain sins, we are afraid that God will leave us as others have., "For He Himself has said, I will never leave you nor forsake you." Hebrews 13:5b

4. We believe that we could never be fully forgiven for our past or present sins., "Then He adds, their sins and their lawless deeds I will remember no more." Hebrews 10:17

We have a hard time seeing God as a loving Father. This is especially true if your relationship with your earthly father was not what it was supposed to be. God is all-powerful and all-knowing, and this may leave us feeling ashamed due to any sin or thoughts that we have been a part of. But God is not emotional, changing His mood based on circumstances. He is Love, never changing, always faithful, and our ever-present help in our times of need.

Hindrances to Knowing God as a Loving Father

Just as Satan lied to Eve in the Garden, he is going to lie to you to make you doubt God's Word. He is on a mission to be sure, to destroy the family unit as we know it. He started with Adam and Eve and made them doubt their Father. He does the same today, making children doubt what their parents say and making people doubt that the promises of

God are for His children. When it comes to our children, if he can make them doubt their parents and adults in general, how will they ever be able to trust their Heavenly Father?

When he twisted the truth and made Eve believe instead of providing everything they needed, God was withholding something that was good for them. How could just a little cause them any harm or cause them to die? A little Leven leavens the whole loaf. A little lie corrupts a man's heart. He will cause you to question God and His love for you just as he tries to make you doubt His provision and kindness towards you. Soon you will start to pull away from God just as Adam and Eve hid in the garden. When this begins to happen, you must resist the devil, and he will flee from you. Draw near to God, and He will draw near to you. James 4:7-8

Do not let what imperfect people do, impact how you see God. His perfect love casts out fear, and where people will likely fail you, God will not fail you.

Removing Barriers to Experiencing God's Love

> "To love at all is to be vulnerable. Love anything, and
> your heart will be wrung and possibly be broken. If
> you want to make sure of keeping it intact, you must
> give it to no one, not even an animal…" – C.S. Lewis

To love is to be vulnerable. If you have ever loved and lost that love, it can be all-consuming. It can cause you to doubt

God's love for you if this happens. The truth is, yes, it hurts; it is real and heartbreaking. Sometimes, we find it hard to receive God's love because we do not see Him physically present. When Jesus left the disciples, He said He would send a Helper, a helper who would be with us always. When we receive Jesus as our Savior, we have access to the Holy Spirit. Through Him, we can experience the true love of God.

We also confuse His love with the way we have experienced human love. When people we love hurt us, we put up a guard to protect our hearts further. Love from people can be fractured and broken. But it can also expose your heart if that person in your life becomes an idol. I can confess that this is me I am referring to. In the last relationship I was in before giving my life back to God, I allowed that person to become an idol. Everything in my life was about wanting to please him and make him happy. He was better than me, I thought. I felt lifted up being in a relationship with him. What I did not realize was that I put so much pressure on him to make me happy when I should have looked to God for that happiness. I needed to know who I was in Christ and let Christ complete me before I could be in a healthy relationship with someone else.

Take a moment and ask God if there is anything in your life right now that has become an idol, anything that is not pleasing to Him, and ask Him to help you to lay it down. When you do this, you will begin to experience more of Him in your life. Only God's love is complete and perfect.

Ways To Receive God's Love

Prayer: One of the most direct ways to experience God's love is through prayer. By communicating with God, we open our hearts to receive His love, guidance, and comfort.

Scripture: God's love is revealed through the scriptures. By studying and reflecting on His Word, we can better understand God's love for humanity.

Nature: Many believe that God's love is evident in the beauty and wonder of the natural world around them. Observing the intricacies of creation can inspire a sense of awe and gratitude for God's love.

Acts of Kindness: God's love is often expressed through the compassion and kindness of others. When we experience love and care from others, it can be seen as a reflection of God's love in our lives.

Personal Experiences: God's love can manifest in personal experiences, such as moments of joy, peace, or comfort during challenging times. These moments can be seen as God's presence and love in our lives.

Forgiveness: Experiencing God's love through forgiveness is powerful. When we seek forgiveness and receive it from others or extend it to those who have wronged us, we can experience God's grace and love in the process.

Relationships: Meaningful and loving relationships with family and friends can also be a way to experience God's love. The blessings of the connection with our family and friends remind us of the price He paid to have a restored relationship with us.

Worship: Worship can help open our hearts to receive God's love and deepen our spiritual connection with Him.

Acts of Service: Expressing love to others through acts of service, charity, and selflessness can help us feel God's love flowing through us and toward those we help.

Remember, the experience of God's love can be deeply personal and can vary from person to person. It is essential to be open to different ways of receiving and recognizing the love of God in our lives.

RESTING IN GOD'S LOVE DURING DIFFICULT TIMES

Be Still and know that I am God. Psalm 46:10a

To be still or to rest in God does not mean to sit and do nothing. You can be physically still, yet your heart and mind are focused on the things going on in your life. To be still is a heart posture that allows your heart to get in line with Him so you can truly rest in His presence. This is something we need to practice because when trouble comes, you need to be able to go before the Lord and be still, allowing Him to comfort and guide you.

Being still in God's love involves prioritizing His love above His judgment. While God is a just judge and should be revered, fixating solely on potential punishment or feelings of disappointment hinders growth. Embracing God's love involves acknowledging His infinite love, grace, and mercy that consistently envelop us, empowering us to thrive in any circumstance.

The benefit of resting in God's love is the resulting changes you see in yourself. As you learn to rest in Him, there is less fear of making mistakes. You begin to make decisions without thinking that God is going to be disappointed in you. Your actions are not dictated by what you imagine other people will think. Your focus is on pleasing God, not man.

Having Faith in Difficult Times

"For by grace you have been saved through faith, and that not of yourself; it is the gift of God." Ephesians 2:8

"For we walk by faith, not by sight." 2 Corinthians 5:7

In times of hardship, such as financial struggles, difficult relationships, health issues, or doubts about our self-worth, it can be challenging to recognize that God is continuously at work within us. As humans, we often rely on what we can see and experience rather than having faith, which is what God encourages us to center our focus on.

Why Having The Gift of Faith Can Save Us

Believing or having faith during challenging periods can lead to serenity in God's company. A lack of faith, on the other hand, can lead to an inflated ego that distances you from your bond with Him. Relinquishing your hardships and issues to God can relieve an immense weight from your shoulders. God has given us a measure of faith, allowing us to perceive His works so that we would remain calm in life's uncertainties instead of constantly worrying.

Principles for Trusting God in Difficult Times

Embrace Faith Over Fear: In challenging times, choosing faith over fear is essential. Trust in God's plan and believe that He will guide you through the obstacles, no matter how insurmountable they may seem.

Surrender Your Control: You must learn to relinquish your control over situations and trust in God's providence. Understand that His ways and timing may not always align with your own, yet they always serve a greater purpose.

Find Strength in Prayer: Regular prayer can serve as a powerful tool during tough times. It not only provides comfort but also strengthens your connection with God, reaffirming your trust in His capabilities.

Seek Wisdom in Scripture: Scriptures contain the wisdom and teachings of God. Studying them can provide guidance during challenging periods, reinforcing your trust in His principles and promises.

Practice Gratitude: Even during tough times, try to maintain an attitude of gratitude. Recognizing and being thankful for God's blessings in your life can nurture a sense of peace and trust in His plan for you.

SHARING GOD'S LOVE WITH OTHERS

Simple Ways to Show God's Love to Others

Listening: Demonstrating God's love through listening means giving someone your full attention, showing empathy, and validating their feelings and experiences. It is not just about hearing words but understanding the emotions behind them. This type of attentive listening reflects God's love and care, conveying to the person that they are important and their experiences matter.

Generosity: Generosity is a practical and tangible way of showing God's love. This can include monetary giving, but it is not limited to that. Generosity can be shown through giving your time, skills, or resources to help others. It reflects the generosity of God, who gives abundantly to all.

Words of Encouragement: The words we speak can have a significant impact on others. Words of encouragement can uplift, motivate, and give hope to people going through tough times. By speaking positively into someone's life, we can reflect the encouraging and affirming nature of God's love.

Acts of Kindness: Acts of kindness can be big or small, but they all reflect God's love in a tangible way. This could be as simple as a smile, a helping hand, or going out of your way to make someone's day better. These acts show the kindness and goodness of God and can significantly impact people's lives.

Praying for Others: Praying for others is a spiritual way of showing God's love. It is an act of selflessness, as you are taking time to intercede on someone else's behalf. It shows your care for them and your belief in God's power to provide, heal, and guide them. It not only benefits the person you are praying for but also helps you develop compassion and empathy.

Bible Verses for Reflection:

- 1 John 4:9-11 - "This is how God showed his love among us: He sent his one and only Son into the world that we might live through him. This is love: not that we loved God, but that he loved us and sent his Son as an atoning sacrifice for our sins. Dear friends, since God so loved us, we also ought to love one another."

- Ephesians 3:17-18 NIV - "so that Christ may dwell in your hearts through faith. And I pray that you, being rooted and established in love, may have power, together with all the Lord's holy people, to grasp how wide and long and high and deep is the love of Christ."
- Zephaniah 3:17 - "The Lord your God is with you, the Mighty Warrior who saves. He will take great delight in you; in his love he will no longer rebuke you but will rejoice over you with singing."
- Psalm 136:26 - "Give thanks to the God of heaven. His love endures forever."

Reflective Questions:

1. How open is my heart to receiving and experiencing God's unconditional love in my life?
2. What fears or barriers might be preventing me from fully opening my heart to God's love, and how can I overcome them?
3. In what ways can I deepen my understanding and awareness of God's love for me, and how can I actively seek to encounter His love in my daily life?
4. How does opening my heart to God's love impact my relationships with others and my ability to extend love and compassion to those around me?
5. What practices or habits can I incorporate into my life to cultivate a deeper sense of connection with

God and to continually open my heart to His transforming love?

As we end this chapter, remember, in the journey to understanding God's boundless and infinite love, we recognize the need to break free from misconceptions about God's love being conditional. As we open our hearts to receive His love, the same capacity to love unconditionally can flow through us. It also addressed the barriers and hindrances to receiving His love, such as lies from the enemy, unforgiveness, and fear, while also providing insights on overcoming these obstacles. Through various means like prayer, scripture, nature, and acts of kindness, we are encouraged to personally and deeply experience God's love, an experience that varies from person to person but consistently leads to inner peace and the ability to love without condition.

Resting in God's love during challenging times involves adopting a heart posture aligned with Him, prioritizing His love over judgment, and finding strength through faith, prayer, and scripture. Being still in God's presence empowers us to thrive, reducing fear and self-consciousness and focusing on pleasing God rather than people. In hardships, it is essential to walk by faith and not sight, trusting in God's plan, surrendering control, and seeking wisdom in His teachings.

As we begin the next chapter on conquering negative self-talk, we will identify the patterns and learn how to transform our negative thoughts through the truth in God's Word. As we begin to understand and to cultivate a positive and Christ-centered mindset, we will overcome the different insecurities and walk in confidence as a believer.

6

CONQUERING NEGATIVE SELF-TALK

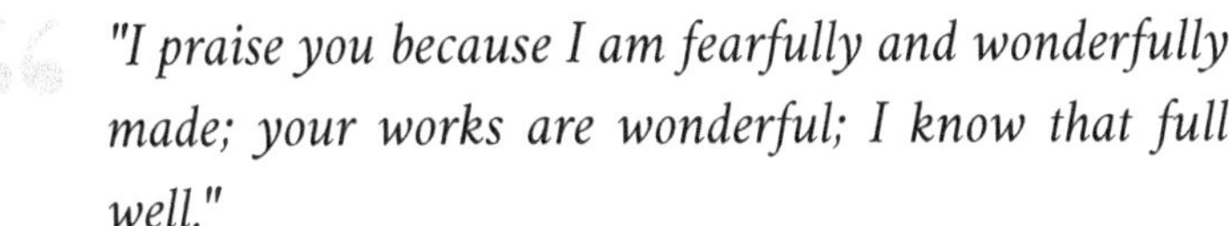

"I praise you because I am fearfully and wonderfully made; your works are wonderful; I know that full well."

— PSALM 139:14

IDENTIFYING AND CHALLENGING NEGATIVE SELF-TALK PATTERNS

What is negative self-talk? It is a line of thought that you begin speaking to yourself that tears down any good quality, reducing your self-worth. Where does this negative self-talk come from? It usually comes from past experiences that became a core part of your inner belief. Negative self-talk can lead to addiction and mental health issues.

Why are we prone to negative thoughts and self-talk? Negative self-talk can be a complex phenomenon influenced by several factors. Here is why many individuals may be prone to it:

- **Childhood Experiences:** Negative self-talk can stem from early experiences with parents, caregivers, or peers that were overly critical or unsupportive. This can lead to internalized beliefs about self-worth and competence.
- **Cultural and Social Influences:** Societal pressures and norms can influence self-talk. Comparing oneself to others or striving for perfection based on societal standards might lead to negative self-assessment.
- **Stress and Anxiety:** During periods of stress and anxiety, people are more likely to engage in negative self-talk. This can create a vicious cycle where negative thoughts increase stress levels, further reinforcing negative self-talk.
- **Low Self-Esteem:** People with low self-esteem may use negative self-talk as a defense mechanism. By expecting the worst, they might feel they are protecting themselves from disappointment.
- **Lack of Mindfulness or Self-Awareness:** Without being conscious of thought patterns and actively working to cultivate positive thinking, negative self-talk can become a default mode of thinking.

In combating negative self-talk, understanding these under-lying causes can be essential. Techniques such as prayer, mindfulness, and self-compassion practices can be effective tools in challenging and transforming negative self-talk into a more balanced and positive internal dialogue.

Examples of negative self-talk are when you blame yourself for things when they go wrong and when there is no factual evidence to back it up. Or when you do make a small mistake, you think the result will be a disaster that you will not be able to overcome. When these things happen, you cannot see any good, only the negative. One small thing can try to ruin your entire day.

If these types of thinking sound familiar, you surely want to know how to stop negative thought cycles in their tracks. When I was younger, I thought I could do anything. As I got older, however, I started listening to what people were saying about what I wanted to do. They would say things like, "what if it does not work out? What if you mess it up? I could not do that because I would be too embarrassed if something went wrong." They were not saying I would fail, but their doubts about what I wanted to do began to make me feel like I could not do it.

When I became a true Christian, God helped me to recognize the thoughts that I was dealing with. He started by making me recognize what was feeding my thoughts. I was dealing with influences from music, television, and some not-so-nice coworkers. The gates to my heart and mind were wide open to anything and everything. I was listening to country music, watching vampires and witches on TV, and listening to some co-workers try to tell me I would not succeed beyond where I was in the company.

We must pay attention to what we are allowing to pass through the gates. We have the power and authority to protect ourselves, mind, body, and spirit. If you have locks on your doors and a fence around your yard, you are protecting your home and property and limiting what passes through. The same focus on protection should happen with your heart and mind. In biblical days, priests would often oversee the gates and maintain the sanctity of the sanctuary. They would control access, ensuring that only those who were properly purified or who had met specific criteria could enter.

When we realize that our bodies are a temple where the Holy Spirit dwells, don't you think we should protect them as we would a treasure of immense value? The best way for us to transform our thinking and protect and renew our minds is through the Word of God. Paul warns us in 2 Corinthians 11:3 that as the serpent (Satan) deceived Eve, he could corrupt our minds. These are the negative thoughts, doubts, and fears that can sometimes overwhelm us.

"But I fear, lest somehow, as the serpent deceived Eve by his craftiness, so your minds may be corrupted from the simplicity that is in Christ." 2 Corinthians 11:3

Paul understands how easily our minds can be corrupted through deception. He was a Pharisee of the strictest sect. He lived his life as a Jew to the highest standard. After the death of Jesus, he went out persecuting and killing Christians because they were following Christ. He was guided by the chief priest to go after those followers of Jesus to stop them from preaching and sharing Jesus. He did all of this without ever knowing or meeting Jesus. Until one day when everything changed, and his life was transformed. That day as he was headed to Damascus with orders and authority from the chief priests, he came face to face with Jesus. The account of Paul's conversion can be found in Acts 26:12-18.

Paul not only had his eyes opened to the calling and purpose that God had for his life during that encounter, but Jesus said He would send him to preach the gospel to the Gentiles, those not belonging to the Jewish community of Faith. Talk about an encounter that caused a 180° change in perspective. When He encountered Jesus, his way of thinking completely changed.

In verse 17, Jesus told him He would deliver him from the Jews, his own people. He was telling him He would keep him safe. Jesus knew that Paul could have a moment to be in fear if he did not continue following the orders of the ones who sent him. However, before Paul could even think or speak of it, Jesus assured him that he would be delivered and that he would open the eyes of the ones he was being sent to.

There are times and opportunities where we will have a moment of doubt about our abilities, talents, and self-worth. But it is imperative that we keep our attention on what the Word of God says. We must not let our guard down and allow our minds and hearts to be filled with garbage.

> Keep your heart with all diligence, for out of it
> springs the issues of life. Proverbs 4:23

Consider the choice and responsibility you have to protect your heart and mind. I always use this example with my kids. If Jesus were in the room with you, would you watch that TV program, would you listen to that music? If Jesus were in the room with you, would He agree with what that person said about you? The answer is a resounding no.

There were several times in the Bible when people came to Jesus to ask for help, and then someone came with a bad report. Before they had a chance to doubt or worry, Jesus told them only believe. What was He telling them to believe? He was telling them to believe what they had heard before. He did not want them to focus on the negative news that came to them but instead what brought them to Him to begin with. They believed He was a Healer, He wanted them to continue believing that He would heal.

WHAT DOES THE BIBLE SAY ABOUT OUR THOUGHTS?

In Romans 7:22-23 Paul explains that he loves God's law with all his heart, but that there is another power at work within him, and it is at war with his mind. (Authors paraphrase). Paul was telling us that our flesh, or sinful nature is at odds with the Word of God. We must be the boss of our bodies and control what we are putting into it. If a person wants to lose weight, they are going to put less sugar and carbs into their body. If they want to strengthen their mind, they are going to read and focus on the things that will build them up. The following verses from the scriptures are a few that help us to understand what we are to do about our thoughts.

"Therefore, I tell you, do not worry about your life, what you will eat or drink; or about your body, what you will wear. Is not life more than food, and the body more than clothes? Look at the birds of the air; they do not sow or reap or store away in barns, and yet your heavenly Father feeds them. Are you not much more valuable than they? Can any one of you by worrying add a single hour to your life?" Mathew 6:25-27 NIV

And do not be conformed to this world, but be transformed by the renewing of your mind, that you may prove what is that good and acceptable and perfect will of God. Romans 12:2

For though we walk in the flesh, we do not war according to the flesh. For the weapons of our warfare are not carnal but mighty in God for pulling down strongholds, casting down arguments and every high thing that exalts itself against the knowledge of God, bringing every thought into captivity to the obedience of Christ. 2 Corinthians 10:3-5

How Do We Overcome Negative Thoughts as a Christian

If we look at 2nd Corinthians 10:3-5, Paul is telling us that our weapons of warfare are not carnal, which means it is not of this world. So, what are the weapons of our warfare?

Paul says finally, my brethren, be strong in the Lord and in the power of His might. Put on the whole armor of God, that you may be able to stand against the wiles of the devil. For we do not wrestle against flesh and blood, but against principalities, against powers, against the rulers of the darkness of this age, against spiritual hosts of wickedness in the heavenly places. Therefore, take up the whole armor of God, that you may be able to withstand in the evil day, and having done all, to stand. Ephesians 6:10-13

What is the Whole Armor of God that Paul is referring to? The Armor of God as described in Ephesians 6:14-17 serves as a metaphor for the spiritual tools and defenses Christians must equip themselves with to stand firm against the strategies and deceptions of the devil. Each piece represents an essential facet of the Christian faith that believers can "put on" in spiritual warfare.

1. Belt of Truth (Ephesians 6:14a)
- Just as a belt holds other pieces of armor together, truth serves as a foundational piece. It symbolizes honesty and integrity. In spiritual warfare, it helps Christians stand against deception, ensuring they are grounded in the reality of God's Word and not swayed by lies or misrepresentations.

2. Breastplate of Righteousness (Ephesians 6:14b)
- A breastplate protects vital organs, especially the heart. Symbolizing purity and the righteousness that comes through faith in Christ, it safeguards believers' hearts from accusations and guilt, reminding them that they are justified by faith, not works.

3. Feet Fitted with the Gospel of Peace (Ephesians 6:15)
- Proper footwear provides stability and readiness. Having one's feet shod with the Gospel of Peace means being prepared to share the good news of Christ, standing firm in faith, and promoting peace.

It enables believers to walk confidently in a world of chaos, knowing they carry the message of peace.

4. Shield of Faith (Ephesians 6:16)
- The shield provides broad protection against attacks. Faith, symbolized by this shield, defends believers against the "flaming arrows" of doubt, temptation, and accusation. By holding up faith, Christians can extinguish these attacks and secure in their trust in God's promises and character. *Additionally, back in the days of the Biblical battles, it is said that the soldiers soaked their wooden shields in water to prevent them from catching fire from the flaming arrows. Verse 16 says, "above all, taking the shield of faith which, you will be able to quench the fiery darts of the wicked one." If it were not saturated in water, their shield would go up in flames.

5. Helmet of Salvation (Ephesians 6:17a)
- A helmet protects the head, a critical part of the body. The helmet represents the assurance of salvation, guarding believers' minds from doubt and securing them in the knowledge that they are saved and redeemed by Christ. It serves as a constant reminder of their eternal security and identity in Him.

6. Sword of the Spirit (Ephesians 6:17b)

- Unlike the other pieces of armor, which are defensive, the sword is an offensive weapon. It represents the Word of God, which is alive and active. In spiritual battles, the Scriptures are the believer's primary tool in both defending against and countering the schemes of the enemy. By knowing and wielding the Word of God, Christians can confront lies, temptations, and spiritual attacks with divine truth.

In the broader context, the Armor of God emphasizes the importance of being spiritually vigilant and prepared. It encourages believers to rely not on their strength but on God's provisions for enduring and resisting spiritual challenges.

WALKING IN CONFIDENCE AND VICTORY OVER NEGATIVE SELF-TALK

In Colossians 2:8 we are told, "Beware lest anyone cheat you through philosophy and empty deceit, according to the tradition of men, according to the basic principles of the world, and not according to Christ." When people speak anything against you that is not according to the Word of God, they are attempting to deceive and cheat you of what God has already given to you.

The NLT Bible says it like this, "Don't let anyone capture you with empty philosophies and high-sounding nonsense that comes from human thinking and from the spiritual powers of this world, rather than from Christ." Think about that for a moment. Don't let anyone capture you or trap you into thinking negative thoughts about yourself. But as 2 Corinthians 10:5 says, take the thoughts captive under the obedience of Christ.

As children of God, we already have the victory. It was secured on our behalf by Christ Jesus's death and resurrection.

"But you belong to God, my dear children. you have already won a victory over those people, because the spirit who lives in you is greater than the spirit who lives in the world." 1 John 4:4 (NLT)

"Even if we feel guilty, God is greater than our feelings, and he knows everything." 1 John 3:20 (NLT)

Walking in confidence and victory over negative self-talk is a crucial aspect of the Christian journey. This involves renewing our minds with the truths of Scripture and applying these truths in our day-to-day lives. Here are some steps and scriptures to help guide you.

1. Understand Your Identity in Christ: Realize that you are deeply loved, chosen, and redeemed by God. This forms the foundation of true self-worth and counters negative self-talk.

"But as many as received Him, to them He gave the right to become children of God, to those who believe in His name." John 1:12

"For you are a holy people to the LORD your God; the LORD your God has chosen you to be a people for Himself, a special treasure above all the peoples on the face of the earth." Deuteronomy 7:6

2. Renew Your Mind: Replace negative thoughts with God's truths by immersing yourself in the Word.

"And do not be conformed to this world, but be transformed by the renewing of your mind, that you may prove what is that good and acceptable and perfect will of God." Romans 12:2

3. Speak God's Word Over Yourself: When negative thoughts arise, combat them with the truth of God's Word.

"Let the word of Christ dwell in you richly in all wisdom, teaching and admonishing one another in psalms and hymns and spiritual songs, singing with grace in your hearts to the Lord." Colossians 3:16

4. Guard Your Heart: Protect your heart from negative influences that can inspire negative self-talk.

"Keep your heart with all diligence, for out of it
spring the issues of life." Proverbs 4:23

5. Stay Connected with Fellow Believers: Surround yourself with believers who encourage, uplift, and remind you of God's truths.

"And let us consider one another in order to stir up
love and good works, not forsaking the assembling of
ourselves together, as is the manner of some, but
exhorting one another, and so much the more as you
see the day approaching." Hebrews 10:24-25

6. Pray Continuously: Ask God for strength and wisdom to combat negative self-talk.

"Be anxious for nothing, but in everything by prayer
and supplication, with thanksgiving, let your
requests be made known to God; and the peace of
God, which surpasses all understanding, will guard
your hearts and minds through Christ Jesus."
Philippians 4:6-7

7. Remember the Power of Christ in You: Recognize that you are not fighting negative self-talk in your own strength but with the power of Christ in you.

> "I can do all things through Christ who strengthens me." Philippians 4:13

8. Rejoice in the Lord Always: Cultivate a heart of gratitude. Rejoicing in the Lord, even amidst challenges, can shift our focus from negative self-talk to God's goodness.

> "Rejoice in the Lord always. Again, I will say, rejoice!" Philippians 4:4

Incorporating these steps and meditating on these Scriptures will help you as a believer to anchor your identity in Christ, combatting the influences of negative self-talk and allowing you to walk in victory.

The benefits of a Christ-centered mindset guides believers in all aspects of their lives. Cultivating this mindset involves intentionality, prayer, immersion in God's Word, and the practice of Christian disciplines. Below are details on the benefits of a Christ-centered mindset and practical ways to embody Christ-centered living.

Benefits of a Christ-Centered Mindset:

1. Peace and Assurance: When Christ is at the center, we can navigate life's challenges with a profound sense of peace, knowing God is in control.

"And the peace of God, which surpasses all understanding, will guard your hearts and minds through Christ Jesus." Philippians 4:7

2. Guidance and Wisdom: By focusing on Christ, we receive guidance and wisdom in our decisions and actions.

"If any of you lacks wisdom, let him ask of God, who gives to all liberally and without reproach, and it will be given to him." James 1:5

3. Strength in Trials: A Christ-centered mindset equips us to endure challenges with resilience and hope.

"Fear not, for I am with you; Be not dismayed, for I am your God. I will strengthen you, Yes, I will help you, I will uphold you with My righteous right hand." Isaiah 41:10 NIV

4. Joy and Contentment: True joy and contentment are found in a relationship with Christ, not in worldly circumstances.

"For the kingdom of God is not eating and drinking, but righteousness and peace and joy in the Holy Spirit." Romans 14:17

How to Practice Christ-Centered Living:

1. Prioritize Daily Devotion: Spend time daily in prayer and studying God's Word to draw closer to Christ.

"But his delight is in the law of the Lord, and in His law, he meditates day and night." Psalm 1:2

2. Seek God's Will in Decisions: Before making choices, seek God's guidance and will.

"Trust in the Lord with all your heart and lean not on your own understanding; In all your ways acknowledge Him, and He shall direct your paths." Proverbs 3:5-6

3. Practice Humility: Consider others before yourself and look for opportunities to serve, reflecting Christ's love to the world.

"Let nothing be done through selfish ambition or conceit, but in lowliness of mind let each esteem others better than himself." Philippians 2:3

4. Join a Community of Believers: Engage in fellowship, worship, and service with other Christians to encourage and be encouraged in the faith.

"And let us consider one another in order to stir up love and good works, not forsaking the assembling of ourselves together, as is the manner of some, but exhorting one another." Hebrews 10:24-25

5. Guard Your Mind and Heart: Be cautious about what you consume, ensuring it aligns with Christ's teachings.

"Finally, brethren, whatever things are true, whatever things are noble, whatever things are just, whatever things are pure, whatever things are lovely, whatever things are of good report, if there is any virtue and if there is anything praiseworthy—meditate on these things." Philippians 4:8

6. Demonstrate Christ's Love: Show kindness, mercy, and love to others as Christ has done for us.

> "A new commandment I give to you, that you love one another; as I have loved you, that you also love one another." John 13:34

By understanding the benefits of a Christ-centered mindset and actively seeking to live with Christ at the center, we can walk in a positive and Christ-centered approach to life that shines God's light into the world.

OVERCOMING INSECURITIES AND COMPARISON

Insecurities. We have all faced them at one point or another. They are those nagging feelings of inadequacy, self-doubt, and often the painful belief that we are not enough. In our Christian walk, it is even more essential to address them, not just for our peace but to live in the fullness of what God intended for us.

What are insecurities? Insecurities are deep-rooted feelings of uncertainty or anxiety about oneself. They manifest as beliefs that we are not up to par, whether in appearance, skills, relationships, or any other aspect of life.

3 Types of Insecurities and the Word of God to Overcome Them

1. Physical Insecurities: Concerns about our appearance, physique, or any physical trait. This might sound like, "I'm not tall enough, thin enough, or attractive enough."

"For You formed my inward parts; You covered me in my mother's womb. I will praise You, for I am fearfully and wonderfully made; Marvelous are Your works, and that my soul knows very well." Psalm 139:13-14

2. Emotional Insecurities: Doubts about our worthiness of love, acceptance, or belonging. It whispers, "I'm unlovable or not good enough."

"But God demonstrates His own love toward us, in that while we were still sinners, Christ died for us." Romans 5:8

3. Performance Insecurities: Feelings that we are not competent or capable enough in our roles, at work, in ministry, or in personal endeavors.

But He said to me, 'My grace is sufficient for you, for My power is made perfect in weakness.' Therefore, I will boast all the more gladly about my weaknesses, so that Christ's power may rest on me. 2 Corinthians 12:9

Consequences of insecurities, if unchecked, can lead to anxiety, depression, jealousy, and a host of other negative emotions. They can also hinder our relationships, making us defensive or overly sensitive. Most importantly, they obstruct our relationship with God, making us question His love, purpose, and promises.

What causes insecurity? Insecurities often sprout from past experiences, rejections, failures, or negative comments that have taken root in our minds. Living in a world that thrives on comparison, especially in the age of social media, only fuels this fire.

Tips to Overcome Insecurities:

1. Recognize and Accept: First, recognize that everyone, yes, everyone, has insecurities. Acceptance is the first step towards healing.

2. Stop the Comparison Game: Every time you catch yourself comparing, halt. Remember, everyone's journey is different.

3. Affirmations: Speak positive affirmations over yourself based on the truths from God's Word.

How to Overcome Insecurity with God's Help:

1. Dive into Scripture: Immerse yourself in God's Word. Let His truths about your identity become louder than the voices of doubt.

2. Pray: Share your feelings with God. Ask Him to heal areas of insecurity and to give you a revelation of His love.

3. Seek Community: Share your struggles with a trusted friend or mentor. They can provide encouragement and a godly perspective.

Helpful Bible Verses To Help You Overcome Insecurity:

1. "For I, the Lord your God, will hold your right hand, Saying to you, 'Fear not, I will help you.'" Isaiah 41:13

2. "The Lord is my light and my salvation; Whom shall I fear? The Lord is the strength of my life; Of whom shall I be afraid?" Psalm 27:1

3. "But you are a chosen generation, a royal priesthood, a holy nation, His own special people, that you may proclaim the praises of Him who called you out of darkness into His marvelous light."1 Peter 2:9

Remember, God created you uniquely and wonderfully. He did not make a mistake. Whenever insecurity whispers, let

God's Word shout louder. Stand firm in His love and promises, and gradually, those insecurities will fade in the light of His truth.

Walking in the world today, it is easy to be swayed by the myriad voices clamoring for our attention. From the pressures of society to the allure of worldly desires, it is an ongoing challenge to remain steadfast. Yet, as believers in the Almighty, we have been given a profound gift that allows us to walk in confidence: our faith in Jesus Christ.

Why is confidence essential for a believer? Confidence does not mean pride or arrogance. Instead, it is about understanding who we are in Christ and standing firm in that identity. It is the deep-seated belief that God is in control, that He has a purpose for our lives, and that He's with us every step of the way.

The Bible tells us, "But as many as received Him, to them He gave the right to become children of God, to those who believe in His name." John 1:12 (NKJV). As God's children, we are co-heirs with Christ. This identity gives us a divine purpose, value, and authority. When we fully grasp this, our perspective shifts and worldly troubles diminish in the face of eternal truths.

God's Word is filled with promises that are yes and amen in Christ. When uncertainty arises, we can stand firm, knowing that God's promises are unwavering. The Scripture reassures us, "Being confident of this very thing, that He who has begun a good work in you will complete it until the day of Jesus Christ." Philippians 1:6 (NKJV). This means that God is actively working in our lives, shaping, and refining us for His glory.

Living a life led by the Holy Spirit empowers us with wisdom, strength, and discernment. As Galatians 5:25 (NKJV) reminds us, "If we live in the Spirit, let us also walk in the Spirit." With the Spirit guiding our steps, we can walk confidently, knowing we are in alignment with God's will.

In a world filled with critics and doubters, it is essential to have a church family that uplifts, encourages, and challenges you in your faith. As Proverbs 27:17 (NKJV) says, "As iron sharpens iron, so a man sharpens the countenance of his friend." Being connected in Christ with your church family will help boost your confidence as you witness God's work in others' lives and share testimonies of His goodness.

Recall the times God has come through for you, the answered prayers, the unexpected blessings, and even the trials where He carried you through. Remembering His faithfulness in the past will bolster your confidence for the future. He is the same yesterday, today, and forever.

Walking in confidence is not about ignoring challenges or hardships. Instead, it is about facing them head-on, equipped with the knowledge that the Creator of the universe is by your side. It is about resting in the shadow of the Almighty, knowing that He will guide, protect, and provide. Continue to immerse yourself in God's Word, for it is the wellspring of truth and confidence. And as you walk this earthly journey, may you always be reminded of the Apostle Paul's words: "For I am persuaded that neither death nor life, nor angels nor principalities nor powers, nor things present nor things to come, nor height nor depth, nor any other created thing, shall be able to separate us from the love of God which is in Christ Jesus our Lord." Romans 8:38-39 (NKJV).

Walk confidently, for you are held, cherished, deeply loved, and empowered by the King of Kings.

Bible Verses for Reflection:

- Genesis 1:27 - "So God created mankind in his own image, in the image of God he created them; male and female he created them."
- Proverbs 18:21 - "The tongue has the power of life and death, and those who love it will eat its fruit."
- Philippians 4:13 - "I can do all this through him who gives me strength."
- Isaiah 43:1 - "But now, this is what the Lord says— he who created you, Jacob, he who formed you, Israel: 'Do not fear, for I have redeemed you; I have summoned you by name; you are mine.'"

Reflective Questions:

1. What recurring negative thoughts or self-talk patterns do I often find myself engaging in, and how

do they impact my self-esteem and overall well-being?

2. What underlying beliefs or past experiences might be contributing to my negative self-talk, and how can I challenge and reframe those beliefs in a more positive and empowering way?

3. How does negative self-talk affect my ability to pursue my goals, take risks, and embrace new opportunities?

4. What strategies or techniques have been effective in helping me combat negative self-talk in the past, and how can I incorporate them into my daily life to build a healthier mindset?

5. How can I cultivate self-compassion and practice self-care as a means of countering negative self-talk and nurturing a more positive and supportive inner dialogue?

As we discussed the ways to conquer negative self-talk, there were several scriptures I repeated throughout this chapter. These verses were foundational, and what I meditated on anytime I felt the heaviness of the battle in my mind. We are not alone in this, as we have a Comforter and Counselor who will strengthen us and guide us every step of the way if we will trust in and lean into His presence and His Word.

But as we pivot to our next chapter, it is crucial to understand that our battle does not end here. The world around us is brimming with snares, and one of its most potent weapons today is social media. As believers, how do we safeguard our minds and hearts in an era dominated by likes, retweets, and ever-shifting trends? How do we discern truth from falsehood amidst the noise? We will look at the profound impact of social media on believers, discern the lies, and jump into God's guidance on navigating this digital age.

7

OVERCOMING THE LIES AND CARES OF THE WORLD

"Do not conform to the pattern of this world, but be transformed by the renewing of your mind. Then you will be able to test and approve what God's will is—his good, pleasing, and perfect will."

— ROMANS 12:2

RECOGNIZING AND ADDRESSING MEDIA INFLUENCES ON SOCIETY TODAY

The pervasive impact of the media on society is undeniable. Its influence permeates our thoughts, perceptions, and behaviors, often subtly molding our worldview. In an era where the lines between truth and falsehood can blur, it is essential to recognize and address the media's role in disseminating both. Overcoming the lies and cares of this world requires a keen understanding of these influences and proactive strategies to navigate them.

The following information is being shared to help us recognize the influence media has on our individual lives. When you recognize their influence, you can take the power back and be selective in your participation. It is so easy to sit and scroll through the inundation of news clips and social media postings and completely lose yourself in the process. This is where we become desensitized to what we are seeing. We think we are just scrolling by, but the images are being captured in our minds like a digital camera with unlimited storage. And when we least expect it, those stored images influence what we buy, what we wear, what we eat, and where we go.

Recognizing Media Influences

1. Agendas and Biases: Every media outlet has its own set of biases and agendas, whether they are openly acknowledged or more covert. These biases can be rooted in political affiliations, commercial interests, or other considerations. A discerning consumer must recognize these slants and take them into account when processing information.

2. Advertisements and Consumerism: Advertising has a profound influence on our desires and values, urging constant consumption and often setting unrealistic standards and ideals that affect our self-esteem and priorities.

3. Social Media and Comparison: Platforms such as Instagram, Facebook, and Twitter can distort reality, leading to feelings of inadequacy as individuals compare their real lives to others' selectively curated highlights.

4. Sensationalism: The drive for higher ratings and clicks has pushed many media outlets towards sensationalism, prioritizing dramatic stories over more nuanced or vital news.

5. Information Overload: With the rise of the digital age and the 24/7 news cycle, we are inundated with information, leading to desensitization, confusion, or heightened anxiety about global events.

Addressing Media Influences

1. Media Literacy Education: Encouraging media literacy programs in schools and communities can help individuals critically assess the messages they receive, evaluate source credibility, and discern fact from fiction.

2. Limit Exposure: Designate times to disconnect from digital devices, social media, and news. Setting boundaries can help maintain mental well-being and perspective.

3. Diversify Your Sources: Relying on a single source or platform for information can create a tunnel vision. By diversifying media consumption, one can gain a more comprehensive and balanced understanding of events.

4. Mindful Consumption: Before accepting or disseminating information, especially on platforms like social media, take a moment to verify its accuracy to prevent the spread of falsehoods.

5. Engage in Direct Conversations: Face-to-face dialogues can offer a depth of understanding that online discussions often lack. Talking with peers about media influences can bring about broader perspectives and shared solutions.

6. Support Trustworthy Media: Lend your support, both vocal and financial, to independent and reputable media outlets that prioritize unbiased, accurate reporting.

7. Mental Health Prioritization: Recognize when media consumption, especially negative or sensationalist content, is impacting your mental health and be prepared to step back or seek support.

In our efforts to overcome the lies and distractions of our world, it is crucial to remember that the power of discernment lies within us. By understanding media influences and making intentional choices in our consumption, we can navigate our globalized society with clarity and purpose.

Why do people share information on social media?

When I first got onto Facebook in 2008 it was because I wanted to stay connected with a group of people that I served with on a mission trip. As the years passed, I continued going back to the same location working with the same people and meeting new people. We all began to be "Friends" through Facebook. This was amazing to me. As each member of the team traveled back and forth, they would share photos of the work that they completed along with pictures of the team. We kept up with the progress of work being completed and each other through this platform. Sounds like this was a great thing, right?

The truth is social media has evolved over the last 15 years from the original function of keeping people connected. People began using Facebook, Twitter, and Instagram as platforms to promote things they supported or believed in. Sounds great, right? I admit, that is how I have shared about this book before it is even completed. I want to share this book because I am passionate about seeing people delivered and set free from the dark or negative thoughts that weigh them down.

What I have had to be mindful of when doing this is to make sure it is not about me. It is about the benefit of God's Word being shared in this book. The tool of social media to promote what you have to offer is far advanced compared to 20 years ago. If you wanted to market or promote something, you had to pay for advertising in a newspaper or TV ad. Now people pay social influencers to promote their products. And how would you choose who you pay to promote for you? You look at the person who has the most followers on the different platforms.

GUARDING YOUR MIND AGAINST THE NEGATIVE MESSAGES

In a world saturated with information, it is increasingly challenging to filter out negative messages. These can come from the media, peers, or even our own inner critic. Over time, these messages can wear down our self-worth and distort our perception of God's love for us. Remember that each one of us grapples with these external and internal negative voices. You are not alone in this struggle.

Dive into the Word of God daily. Scriptures serve as a powerful reminder of God's unwavering love and our inherent worth in His eyes. Set aside quiet moments for reflection and prayer, asking God to guide your thoughts and give you strength. It can be challenging to sit still to pray and read the Word because the result is change. Change in habits, change in thinking, and change in what we do without even thinking. And this last change is key, what we do without even thinking.

I am sure you have heard the phrase "mindlessly scrolling through social media." Ask yourself how often you sit and look at a phone screen, tablet or pc and just keep scrolling. Your thumb is trained on your phone to just keep the data moving. And as much as you think you are not paying much attention to it; your mind still captured the information and within a split second you decided to keep scrolling from data byte to data byte. It can be mind-numbing when you spend so much time looking at social media. And that is the point. If your mind is numb, you will not guard and protect it from the mental attack of the enemy.

You must consider what you are putting into your mind on a regular basis. If you feed it a regular diet of the Word of God to help strengthen it, it will be stronger to defend against the negative messages that are coming at you continually.

Guarding Your Mind in Today's Connected World

With smartphones at our fingertips and the allure of constant connectivity, distractions are endless. The barrage of information can lead to anxiety, overwhelm, and a diminished ability to be present in our lives and relationships. It's only human to feel swept up by the rapid pace of today's digital age. Remember, it is okay to feel overwhelmed, and it is okay to seek moments of stillness.

Designate tech-free hours or days to reconnect with the world around you and build deeper connections with loved ones. Invest in quality time with friends and family, purposing to be present with them. Get out of the house and take walks and enjoy the world around you. Play board games and enjoy the fellowship. And give thanks as you recognize the blessing all around you.

Participate in group studies or workshops that discuss the balance of faith and technology in our lives. Engage in online Christian communities or groups that offer support, positive dialogue, and spiritual nourishment.

Combating the Negative Effects of Social Media

Social media, while a tool for connection, often amplifies feelings of inadequacy, envy, and loneliness. Constant comparison can erode our sense of self and divert our attention from our faith journey. If you have felt diminished joy or rising anxiety because of social media, know that many share your sentiments. Every 'perfect' post you see is but a snippet of someone's life, not their whole reality. You are only seeing what they want you to see. And many times, what you see is through a filter.

Use social media as a platform for spreading love, positivity, and God's word, becoming a beacon of light in a some-times-cloudy digital landscape. In all these areas, remember that our faith offers a wellspring of guidance and strength. By turning to God, seeking community support, and being proactive in our choices, we can navigate these struggles with grace and purpose.

SEEKING TRUTH IN GOD'S WORD AMIDST A WORLD OF DISTRACTIONS

John 10:10 says, "The thief does not come except to steal, and to kill, and to destroy. I have come that they may have life and that they may have it more abundantly." These are letters in red which indicate they are the words of Jesus. He is telling us the thief comes to kill, steal, and destroy, but what is the thief coming to steal, kill, and destroy? He is coming to steal, kill, and destroy the abundant life that Christ has for you. If he can distract you, he can work to defeat you and destroy your life in Christ.

Look at the word distraction. The purpose of distraction is to divide our attention. It prevents us from concentrating.

- The Latin prefix "dis" is to reverse force, apart or away.
- Traction is the action of drawing a body, vehicle, train, or the like, along a surface as a road, track, railroad, or waterway.
- In other words, it is getting your footing to move in one direction

When you get traction in the word of God, it is moving you in the direction of the Lord. A distraction takes your mind away from concentrating on the Word of God. When you get traction in the Word, you become stronger, and your faith grows. Your confidence increases, and you begin to see yourself as God sees you. When this happens, you can be sure the devil is going to come and do whatever he can to distract you or take away your attention from the Word.

Let us look at Martha and Mary, two sisters that Jesus visited, as told in Luke 10:38-42. Martha invited Jesus to her home. She knew Who He was, and she knew the importance of His message. As she prepared to serve him, she was busy and distracted with much work and noticed her sister Mary was sitting at His feet, listening to every word He said. She asks Jesus to send her back to the kitchen to help her because she is having to do everything herself.

> "And Jesus answered and said to her, "Martha, Martha, you are worried and troubled about many things. But one thing is needed, and Mary has chosen that good part, which will not be taken away from her. "Luke 10:41-42

Martha, I am certain, wanted everything to be perfect for her guests. However, she was so focused on the work to be done that she was missing the blessing of fellowship with Jesus. And because Mary chose to listen to Jesus, He said she made the right choice.

Let me be clear, I understand as a mother of three kids, there is a lot of work to be done to clean your house when you have guests coming. In some cases, there might be a pile at the top of my stairs where everything gets taken to, to be sorted later, because we were cleaning "Company is coming" fast. Yes, that is a cleaning speed in our house.

Some days, I have to close my eyes while I sit in my chair in prayer not to be distracted by Legos, coloring books and crayons, or any number of books scattered around my living room. If I do not close my eyes, I will be tempted to get up and start cleaning. But I learned to do this because, when I take my eyes off those things and focus on my Creator, He can order my steps to get all of those things done even faster. And sometimes He reminds me I need to teach my kids they are responsible to put those things away.

Verses about distraction

"No temptation has overtaken you except such as is common to man; but God is faithful, who will not allow you to be tempted beyond what you are able, but with the temptation will also make the way of escape, that you may be able to bear it." 1 Corinthians 10:13

I will meditate on your precepts and contemplate your way. Psalms 119:15

Finally, brethren, whatever things are true, whatever things are noble, whatever things are just, whatever things are pure, whatever things are lovely, whatever things are of good report, if there is any virtue and if there is anything praiseworthy - meditate on these things. Philippians 4:8

Set your minds on things above, not on earthly things. Colossians 3:2

I say then: walk in the Spirit, and you shall not fulfill the lust of the flesh. For the flesh lust against the

Spirit, and the Spirit against the flesh; and these are contrary to one another so that you do not do the things that you wish. Galatians 5:16-17

"No weapon formed against you shall prosper, and every tongue which rises against you in judgment You shall condemn. This is the heritage of the servants of the Lord, and their righteousness is from Me," says the Lord. Isaiah 54:17

Signs of spiritual distraction

1. **An Urge to Settle or Concede** - Sometimes, when we are not surrounded by the right council, we can be encouraged to make choices that are not in line with God's will. If we become desensitized to the ways of this world, we will concede to the lies of Satan, much like Eve did.

2. **Emotional Exhaustion** - Overextending ourselves with too many commitments leaves us feeling emotionally exhausted because we do not say no to some requests. God gave us an example for working, you must take a rest.

3. **Consistent Strain in Relationships** - 1 Peter 3:8 says, "Finally all of you be of one mind, having compassion for one another; love as brothers, be tenderhearted, be courteous." Let love lead in everything you do. Love the sinner but hate the sin.

4. **Increasing Ego or Arrogance** - When we begin to shine and get recognition for what we do, pride can creep in. We lose focus on doing all things unto Christ and begin to focus on our accomplishments and what we do in our own strength. When this happens, we will feel the shift from the presence of God.

5. **Feelings of Guilt** - The first feelings of guilt were felt in the garden when Adam and Eve hid from the Lord. If you feel like you must hide something from the Lord or others, it does not belong in your life. We must renew our minds according to Romans 12:2 regarding the things we say and do.

6. **Resistance to change** - Sometimes, we get comfortable in what we are doing, even in the things we are doing for the Lord. When we resist letting go of those things, it makes it harder for the Lord to help us grow into the bigger plans He has for us.

If we want to stay close to God, then we must guard our hearts, our devotions, and our desires. Matthew 15:18 says, "But the things that come out of a person's mouth come from the heart, and these defile them." Matthew 6:21 adds to that with, "For where your treasure is, there your heart will be also." Whatever you invest most of your time, talent, and treasure (finances) in, that is where your heart is. When you make God and spending time with Him in His Word a priority, He can order your steps to accomplish more than you can imagine.

Our devotion to God is evident in the way we live to obey and honor Him. In other cultures, when someone worships their deity or gods, they make sacrifices or offerings, but it is only an outward display. It is not about any impact or change to the person's heart. God desires obedience over sacrifice, according to 1 Samuel 15:22.

Our desires can point us to God or pull us away from Him. Anything we desire more than Him becomes an idol to us. When we seek God and His kingdom first, He will provide all that we need, according to Matthew 6:33.

CULTIVATING A KINGDOM OF GOD MINDSET

Cultivating a Kingdom of God mindset amidst a worldly culture is about aligning one's values, perspectives, and actions with the teachings of Jesus Christ and the Word of God. It means prioritizing God's will and seeking to reflect His character in every area of our lives. Not only did He give His Word as a guide to how and what we should do. He also gave us the Holy Spirit to help encourage us in our walk.

All Scripture is given by inspiration of God and is profitable for doctrine, for reproof, for correction, for instruction in righteousness, that the man of God may be complete, thoroughly equipped for every good work. 2 Timothy 3:16-17

The New Living Translation states it like this:
All scripture is inspired by God and is useful to teach us what is true and to make us realize what is wrong in our lives. It corrects us when we are wrong and teaches us to do what is right. God uses it to prepare and equip his people to do every good work. 2 Timothy 3:16-17 NLT

Here are some steps to cultivate a kingdom mindset:

1. **Seek First the Kingdom:** As Jesus said in Matthew 6:33, "But seek first the kingdom of God and his righteousness, and all these things will be added to you." Prioritize your spiritual growth and relationship with God.
2. **Study Scripture:** Regularly read and meditate on the Bible. It offers guidance, wisdom, and a foundation for understanding God's Kingdom. Refer to 2 Timothy 3:16-17
3. **Prayer and Meditation:** Communicate with God regularly as this deepens your relationship with Him, helps you discern His will, and strengthens your mind.

4. **Limit Secular Influences:** Be discerning about media consumption and other cultural influences that may divert your focus from Godly principles.

5. **Maintain a Humble Heart:** Recognize God as the source of all wisdom and strength. Be open to correction and learning.

6. **Embrace Perseverance and Patience:** Understand that trials and challenges are part of the Christian journey. They refine faith and develop character.

7. **Cultivate Godly Relationships:** Build and maintain relationships that encourage spiritual growth and are rooted in mutual respect and love. Accountability in these relationships also serves to make you stronger in your faith.

8. **Set Boundaries:** Know when to say no and establish boundaries that protect your spiritual well-being.

9. **Act with Integrity:** Let your actions mirror your faith. Live in a manner consistent with the teachings of Christ.

10. **Share the Gospel:** Embrace opportunities to share the good news with others, letting your life be a testament to God's love and grace.

Remember, the Kingdom of God mindset is counter cultural. It often challenges societal norms and values, but it promises peace, purpose, and eternal significance. As believers navigate worldly culture, it is vital to stay rooted in faith and consistently seek God's direction.

Proverbs 3:5-8 gives great wisdom to guide you in this. "Trust in the Lord with all your heart and lean not on your own understanding; and all your ways acknowledge Him, and he shall direct your path. Do not be wise in your own eyes; fear the Lord and depart from evil. It will be health to your flesh and strength to your bones." Trust in Him and He will direct your steps.

The Undeniable Truths About The Kingdom of God

We have discovered what is necessary to have a Kingdom Mindset. We understand that God is the King and ruler, we are the citizens, and the Law or rule of the land is His Word. When we accept Christ Jesus as our Savior, we become citizens of His Kingdom. We learn the rules, and we follow them. Entrance into this Kingdom is for all people throughout the world. It is not separated by nation or any other earthly boundaries.

It requires a response. The message of Jesus calls for repentance and belief in His death and resurrection. Entering the Kingdom is not just about passive belief but about active faith and transformation.

Entrance is through grace. While human response and transformation are important, entrance into the Kingdom is a gift from God, given through grace and not earned by human effort. It is characterized by righteousness, peace, and joy. These are often cited as marks of the Kingdom, especially based on passages like Romans 14:17.

Do you know how some things are just felt rather than seen? That is the Kingdom of God for you. It is not something physical you can touch, but it is totally there, living inside each of us. Think of it as that inner compass guiding our spiritual journey. Even though it does not have, say, geographical borders, the Kingdom still has its territory.

Access to the Kingdom of God is for everyone, but because of His great love for you, He gave each and every person their own free will. You have the choice to live for Him or not. Just as The Prodigal Son had access to his inheritance and was able to do whatever he wanted to with it, you have that same right. You can accept the inheritance of the Lord as part of his family, or you can live as you want in the world.

The inner transformation takes place when you invite Jesus into your heart. Jesus does not just stay in the background. He is right there with you, guiding you every step as you allow Him to. Here's the thing: it's not about ticking boxes or following a strict protocol. It is like having a best friend in God, where it is all about the relationship and getting your own personal revelation, not just going through the motions.

Keeping and Living with a Kingdom Mindset

> For a time will come when they will no longer
> endure sound doctrine, but according to their own
> desires, because they have itching ears, they will
> Heap up for themselves teachers; and they will turn
> their ears away from the truth and be turned aside to
> fables. But you be watchful in all things, endure
> afflictions, do the work of an evangelist, fulfill your
> ministry. 2 Timothy 4:3-5

A kingdom mindset as a Christian means to view and live your life like Christ's example and not as the world. When we repent and ask for the forgiveness of our sins and begin to live our lives to honor God and all that we say and do, we become a living example of Christ to the world.

A kingdom mindset is also an eternal mindset. It is a mindset that understands that this physical world we live in is not all there is. There is a heavenly realm that cannot be seen with natural eyes but only by the Spirit through the Word of God. When you have a kingdom mindset, you live and do all things with a focus on the eternal outcome.

> "While we do not look at the things which are seen,
> but at the things which are not seen. For the things
> which are seen are temporary, but the things which
> are not seen are eternal." 2 Corinthians 4:18

You live in a way that would not cause your brother to stumble. You live a life that points to God because you realize that Heaven and Hell are very real. Friends and family matter in a different way as you begin to care about their souls and where they will spend eternity when they take their last breath.

Bible Verses for Reflection:

- Philippians 4:8 - "Finally, brothers and sisters, whatever is true, whatever is noble, whatever is right, whatever is pure, whatever is lovely, whatever is admirable—if anything is excellent or praiseworthy—think about such things."
- John 17:17 - "Sanctify them by the truth; your word is truth."
- 1 John 2:15 - "Do not love the world or anything in the world. If anyone loves the world, love for the Father is not in them."
- Matthew 6:33 - "But seek first his kingdom and his righteousness, and all these things will be given to you as well."

Reflective Questions:

1. How have the lies and cares of the world influenced my thoughts, beliefs, and actions, and in what ways have they hindered my personal growth and spiritual journey?

2. What specific lies or negative influences have I allowed to have power over me, and how can I actively challenge and reject them in favor of embracing truth and authenticity?

3. How does my attachment to worldly concerns and opinions impact my peace of mind, joy, and ability to fully trust in God's guidance and provision?

4. In what ways can I cultivate a mindset of discernment and wisdom to recognize the lies and cares of the world, and intentionally choose to align my thoughts and actions with God's truth instead?

5. What practices, disciplines, or habits can I develop to safeguard my heart and mind from the negative influences of the world, and to intentionally fill my life with God's Word, love, and grace?

In the digital age, media plays a significant role in shaping our perceptions, sometimes subtly directing our thoughts and actions. Navigating the fine line between reality and falsehood becomes challenging due to the biases, sensationalism, and information overload presented by various media outlets. It is essential, now more than ever, to remain discerning, recognizing the deep influence the media has on our lives. Whether it is the inherent agendas in news outlets or the carefully curated lives showcased on social media platforms, these influences can subtly alter our perspectives, values, and even our self-worth.

Social media, once a tool for connection, has evolved into a platform for self-promotion, influencing decision-making, and even altering perceptions. While it has its benefits, it also comes with the peril of mindless consumption, leading individuals to a state of numbness where they unconsciously absorb a multitude of messages. This passive intake of information can weaken the mind's defenses against negative influences.

But there is a beacon of hope: the Word of God. Regularly diving into scriptures offers solace and reminds individuals of their value, offering strength to resist these negative influences. By cultivating a mindful approach to media consumption and grounding oneself in truths like God's teachings, individuals can successfully navigate the complexities of the modern world, protecting their minds from the constant barrage of information and staying true to their core beliefs and values.

Navigating the virtual world requires balance. While technology and social media can offer connections, they can also be sources of comparison, envy, and feelings of inadequacy. By being mindful of our digital consumption and prioritizing face-to-face interactions, we can foster genuine relationships and nurture our mental well-being.

But as much as we need to guard against external influences, it is crucial to safeguard against our own inner critic. Drawing strength from biblical stories, like that of Martha and Mary, we are reminded of the essence of true fulfillment. In our quest for perfection, be it in hospitality or other endeavors, it is easy to miss out on the true blessings that lie before us. By focusing on God, we can discern the genuine from the counterfeit and resist distractions that aim to divert us from our path.

To truly overcome the world's lies and cares, it is pivotal to regularly refuel our spirit with God's truth, build genuine connections, and cultivate a discerning heart. In doing so, we stand firm against the world's distortions, ensuring our minds remain anchored in God's purpose and love.

CONCLUSION

As this book ends, let us take a moment to reflect on the profound truths we have uncovered together. The essence of self-discovery, as explored in these chapters, is not merely a quest to understand oneself better. It is an intimate, spiritual journey that can only find its deepest revelations through God's lens.

Your very identity is not just a product of worldly experiences or labels society places upon you; it is a divine testament to how God perceives you. Every individual is unique, treasured, and, above all, loved infinitely by our Creator. Understanding this can provide a foundation stronger than any challenge or doubt that life throws our way.

Past traumas and pain, though undeniably challenging, can be healed through God's grace. By turning to Him, we find solace and strength that transcends our worldly understanding, allowing us to emerge resilient with a spirit fortified by divine love. It is crucial to comprehend that forgiveness, both for us and others, is not just a noble act. It is a liberating step, freeing us from chains of bitterness and resentment and allowing God's love to flow through us more freely.

Opening our hearts might seem like a vulnerable act, especially when past experiences have taught us to guard them fiercely. Yet, by letting God's unwavering love in, we fortify our hearts in ways we could not have fathomed. This divine love serves as a shield, protecting us from the pitfalls of negative self-talk and the constant bombardment of media influences. Instead of getting swayed by external voices, we learn to tune into the gentle whisper of God, guiding us toward our truest selves.

The journey towards discovering who we are in Christ and seeking God's perfect will in our life may not always be easy, but it is worth all the effort. Remember, you are not alone in your walk with God. He is always there to guide you, even when the path may seem uncertain!

In a world filled with chaos and clamor, understanding who you are in Christ Jesus offers an anchoring truth. You are cherished. You are invaluable. And you are loved more than you can ever imagine. As you move forward, remember that this book is not just a guide but a testament to God's eternal love for you. Embrace this truth, live it, and let it guide your every step towards the radiant future God has planned for you.

Thank you for taking the time to read "Who Do You Think You Are?" and for considering leaving a review to support it. I am deeply grateful for your engagement and support.

Wishing you continued peace, hope and love.

Warm regards,
Lorie Eubank

COPYRIGHT NOTICES:

NKJV

Scripture taken from the New King James Version®. Copyright © 1982 by Thomas Nelson. Used by permission. All rights reserved. All Scripture quotations, unless otherwise indicated, are taken from the Holy Bible, New King James Version®.

NIV

Scripture quotations marked (NIV) are taken from the Holy Bible, New International Version®, NIV®. Copyright © 1973, 1978, 1984, 2011 by Biblica, Inc.™ Used by permission of Zondervan. All rights reserved worldwide. www.zondervan.comThe "NIV" and "New International Version" are trademarks registered in the United States Patent and Trademark Office by Biblica, Inc.™

NLT

Scripture quotations marked (NLT) are taken from the *Holy Bible*, New Living Translation, copyright ©1996, 2004, 2015 by Tyndale House Foundation. Used by permission of Tyndale House Publishers, Carol Stream, Illinois 60188. All rights reserved.

REFERENCES

Your Identity in Christ: How God sees you | Cru. (n.d.). Cru.org. https://www.cru.org/us/en/train-and-grow/spiritual-growth/core-christian-beliefs/identity-in-christ.html

Project, J. F. (2023, April 18). 5 tips for finding your Purpose in Christ - Jesus Film Project. *Jesus Film Project.* https://www.jesusfilm.org/blog/finding-purpose-in-christ/

Ong, G. (2022). How to walk in God's promises and wait for them. *Thir.st.* https://thirst.sg/how-to-walk-in-gods-promises-and-wait-for-them/

5 reasons God's grace is sufficient for you even in the darkness - Topical studies. (2022, December 22). biblestudytools.com. https://www.biblestudytools.com/bible-study/topical-studies/5-reasons-god-s-grace-is-sufficient-for-you-even-in-the-darkness.html

Ministries, R. (n.d.). *Moving past regret — Family fire.* Family Fire. https://familyfire.com/articles/moving-past-regret

Letting Go Of Guilt and Regret — Hope for the Broken-Hearted. (n.d.). Hope for the Broken-Hearted. https://www.hopeforthebrokenhearted.com/letting-go-of-guilt-and-regret-1

Inner Healing 101: Healing emotional wounds. (n.d.). https://www.greatbiblestudy.com/emotional-healing/inner-healing-101-healing-emotional-wounds/

The Power of a Praying® Wife - Kindle edition by Omartian, Stormie. Religion & Spirituality Kindle eBooks @ Amazon.com. (n.d.). https://a.co/d/iUD4V8l

Why we should extend grace to others | Cru. (n.d.). Cru.org. https://www.cru.org/us/en/blog/help-others-grow/mentoring/extend-grace-others.html

How To Forgive Others the Way God Forgives Us | Cru. (n.d.). Cru.org. https://www.cru.org/us/en/blog/life-and-relationships/hardships/forgiven-much.html

Admin. (2023, February 23). *The Power of Forgiveness - I Need A Word.* I

Need a Word. https://ineedaword.org/the-power-of-forgiveness-understanding-what-the-bible-says/

Harling, B. (2021). How to understand and internalize God's deep love for us. *Crosswalk.com.* https://www.crosswalk.com/faith/spiritual-life/how-to-understand-and-internalize-gods-deep-love-for-us.html

Maulding, M. (n.d.). *Removing barriers to experiencing God's love.* https://www.gracelifeinternational.com/removing-barriers-to-experiencing-gods-love

Jenkins, J. M. (2021). Overcoming Obstacles to Receiving and Responding to God's Love. *J. Marshall Jenkins.* https://www.jmarshalljenkins.com/2019/10/01/overcoming-obstacles-receiving-responding-gods-love/

Footprints To Recovery Addiction Treatment Centers. (2023). 7 Ways to Combat Negative Self-Talk. *Footprints to Recovery.* https://footprintstorecovery.com/blog/combat-negative-self-talk/

Lebow, H. I. (2021, June 7). *How to let go of negative thoughts: 4 steps.* Psych Central. https://psychcentral.com/depression/letting-go-of-negative-thoughts

Ling, M. (2021, February 25). *How to overcome negative thoughts as a Christian | Truthfully, Michelle.* Truthfully, Michelle. https://truthfullymichelle.com/how-to-overcome-negative-thoughts-as-a-christian/

What does the Bible say about distractions? (n.d.). https://www.openbible.info/topics/distractions

Turningpoint. (2022, March 24). *6 Signs that you're distracted from God's Will - David Jeremiah blog.* David Jeremiah Blog. https://davidjeremiah.blog/6-signs-that-youre-distracted-from-gods-will/

Contributor. (2018, April 17). *How Do I Stay Close to God in A World Full of Distractions? - YMI.* YMI. https://ymi.today/2018/04/how-do-i-stay-close-to-god-in-a-world-full-of-distractions/

How can we have an eternal mindset here on Earth? - Topical studies. (2023, May 19). biblestudytools.com. https://www.biblestudytools.com/bible-study/topical-studies/how-can-we-have-an-eternal-mindset-here-on-earth.html